# A Man With A Big Heart

## *An Angel Among Us*

**By**

**Annette Ramirez**

**To Published by B-Global Publishing**


This book may be purchased for educational, business, or promotional sales. Special discounts are available on quantities purchased by corporations, associations, and others. For more information or to order additional copies of this book, contact the publisher at the address above.
Orders by U.S. trade bookstores and wholesalers.
Email support_staff@drbglobal.net

ISBN:978-1-963980-23-3

B-Global Publishing brings authors to your live event.
For more information or to book an event, contact
support_staff@drbglobal.net



Manufactured and printed in the United States of America and distributed globally by B-Global Publishing.

# Table of Contents

# Dedication

◆◆◆ ══════ ◇ ══════ ◆◆◆

This book is lovingly dedicated to my father, Ernesto Ramirez —
a man whose heart was bigger than life itself.
To the one who taught me strength through quiet courage,
joy through childlike wonder,
and love through unwavering presence. You showed me what it means
to give without limits,
to laugh without apology,
and to lead with humility, humor, and grace.

Thank you for every memory, every adventure,
every early-morning knock on the hotel door,
every shared laugh in the dark during movie nights,
every carnival ride, and every tender moment of care.
You didn't just raise us —
you nurtured us, protected us, celebrated us,
and loved us into the people we are today.
Your legacy lives in every story told,
every smile remembered, every heart you touched,
and in the generations who carry your spirit forward.

This book is for you —
to honor your life, your love, and your beautiful soul.
Thank you for being our hero on earth and our angel in heaven.
We love you forever.

— Annette

# Acknowledgments

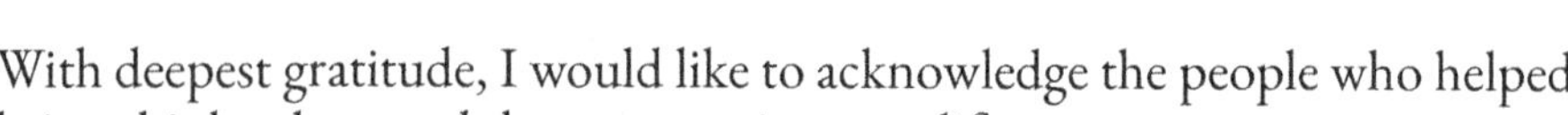

With deepest gratitude, I would like to acknowledge the people who helped bring this book — and these memories — to life.

First and foremost, to my beloved father, Ernesto Ramirez, whose love, laughter, guidance, and joyful spirit shaped not only my childhood, but the woman I am today. Every story in these pages is a piece of his heart — and I am forever blessed to call him my dad.

To my beautiful mother, whose strength, grace, and devotion carried our family through life's joys and sorrows. Your partnership with Dad created a home filled with love, protection, and unforgettable memories. Thank you for always showing us what resilience and unconditional love look like.

To my brother Jimmy, whose life touched us deeply and whose memory lives in every corner of our hearts. Though your time here was brief, the love remains eternal. We carry you with us, always.

To my daughter Lori, the light of our family and the joy of my father's later years. You gave him new purpose, laughter, and so many beautiful moments. Watching the love between you and your grandfather is one of my greatest blessings.

To my family, relatives, and friends who shared in our adventures, vacations, movie nights, and countless special moments — thank you for being part of the memories that shaped our lives.

To everyone who ever experienced my father's kindness, humor, loyalty, and gentle strength — thank you for remembering him with me. Your stories, love, and memories helped me relive the magic of his life and gave me the courage to put it on paper.

Finally, to every reader holding this book — thank you. Thank you for allowing me to share my heart, my stories, and my father's legacy with you. May his life touch yours the way it has touched ours.

# About the Author
# A Legacy Preserved

By Annette Ramirez

My name is Annette Ramirez, daughter of Ernesto and Ann Ramirez, sister to Jimmy, and the proud mother of my greatest blessing on earth — my daughter, Lori.

Before I ever understood legacy, love, or the power of a father's example, I was a little girl growing up on Stewart Street, a place filled with memories, neighbors who became family, and a childhood shaped by simplicity, faith, and the affectionate presence of a man with a heart bigger than Texas.

## My Early Years & Education

I grew up in Laredo, Texas, where I attended Young's Private School, Ryan Elementary, Lamar Middle School, and later graduated from J.W. Nixon High School. My school years gave me strong friendships, teachers who believed in me, and a sense of identity rooted in community.

I later attended college and earned a degree in Fashion Merchandising — a degree that my daughter Lori jokingly refers to as my "degree in shopping," a title I proudly accept. Fashion has always been one of the ways I express joy, personality, and creativity. To me, clothing is art you can wear — and life is always worth dressing beautifully for.

## My Daughter, My Pride

Among everything I have ever done in my life, my daughter Lori is my greatest accomplishment. She has been my companion, my joy, my reason, and the steady reminder of how deeply God has blessed me. Watching her become a mother, a professional, a leader, and a reflection of all the love poured into her has been my life's greatest reward.

## The Grandchildren Who Filled My Heart

Becoming a grandmother has given me a new kind of love — one that is soft, overwhelming, and unconditional.

Adrian, my oldest, is now a sophomore at Alexander High School. He joined the barbecue team and has become a little chef in his own right — grilling steaks that would make any Texan proud.

His confidence, leadership, and kindness make me so proud.

Then came the twins, Lullah Bella and Miguel, seventh graders at Mary Help of Christians School.

Miguel... oh, Miguel. Anyone who meets him immediately sees it — he is my father all over again. Gentle, sweet, intuitive, compassionate. Growing up, when I asked him his name, he proudly said, "Miguel Jellybean!" because that was what I always called him — and he genuinely believed it was his full name. His innocence and joy remind me every day of my dad's heart.

Lullah Bella, on the other hand, is our miracle girl. She is the child we prayed for — the blessing we waited for — and even before she was born, Lori knew exactly what her name would be. My father called Lori "Lullah Bella" all her life, and naming his granddaughter after that nickname became the most beautiful way to honor him.

Every time I say her name, I feel my father close.

## A Life Enriched Through Travel

Travel has always brought me joy — not just the places themselves but the memories made with family. I've been blessed to walk through places so beautiful they feel like dreams.

## Mykonos, Greece

White-washed buildings with blue rooftops that look like a postcard. I fell in love with their narrow paths, sea breezes, and the simplicity of island life. While there, I had the honor of meeting the designer behind Constantino Jewelers, whose artistry left me in awe.

## Barcelona, Spain

I had the privilege of traveling with Lori and her family — watching them explore Gaudí's architecture, stroll through Las Ramblas, and fall in love with Spain one step at a time.

## Rome, Italy

A city of history, faith, and eternal beauty. While Lori and I admired the art and architecture, the boys enjoyed one of their favorite activities — shopping with their grandmother.

## Alaska

A piece of heaven on earth. I will never forget flying on a small plane and landing on water. The cool air, the mountains, the peaceful silence — breathtaking.

## Venice, Italy & Vienna, Austria

Vienna in December was magical — a city floating on glittering water, wrapped in the romance of Christmas lights. My cousin Diane and I traveled to Vienna, and it was a trip that took our breath away. The architecture, the music, the Christmas markets — unforgettable.

These journeys filled my heart, opened my eyes to beauty beyond borders, and reminded me that life is meant to be lived fully. While I can, I plan to see more of the world. Every adventure becomes another chapter of gratitude.

## Why I Wrote This Book

Although this section is "About the Author," the truth is... everything about me leads back to my father.

I wrote this book not just to tell his story but to preserve it — to ensure that long after I am gone, and long after my grandchildren grow up, his love, his character, his humor, and his goodness will still live on.

This book captures:

- the historical roots of our Bruni and Henry lineage
- the humble beginnings that shaped him
- the bond between siblings
- the heartbreak of losing a child
- the innocence and humor he carried
- the love story with my mother
- the adventures that made us who we are
- the legacy of faith and generosity he passed down
- the final days we walked him home
- the way he continues loving us from heaven

I wanted to document both the history and the heart — the facts and the feelings — so that future generations will know exactly who he was.

A man of integrity.
A man of humility.
A man of generosity.
A man with a heart bigger than Texas

As his daughter, I feel responsible — honored, truly — to ensure his story is not forgotten. This book is my way of keeping him alive not only in memory but in the legacy we hand to the next generation.

## A Final Word Before the Introduction

As you turn the page into the Introduction, I invite you to take this journey with me — a journey through love, courage, loss, faith, and the kind of man the world doesn't make anymore.

This is not just my father's story.
It's a story of family, resilience, grace, and the beauty of a life lived well.

I wrote this book with all my heart... because he lived his whole life giving all of his.

.

# Introduction

## Why This Book Was Written — and Why Now

### A Daughter's Promise to Preserve a Legacy

There are moments in life when we carry a story inside us for so long that it becomes part of our heartbeat. For years, this book lived quietly within me — forming itself through memories, conversations, grief, healing, and the unshakable love I feel for my father, Ernesto Ramirez.

Many times I wanted to begin writing.
Many times I tried.
But God has His timing... and His timing is always perfect.

For five years, I carried this desire to honor my father in a written legacy. I even sat with Father Anthony, who encouraged me gently, "Annette, sit down and write.

When God is ready, He will open the door."

For a long time, the words didn't come.
I wasn't ready.

But life brought seasons of hardship. Moments when I felt lost, unseen, and aching for strength. In those valleys, I felt my father's presence the most. His love became the anchor that held me steady, and I realized...

It was time.
Time to heal.
Time to honor the man who shaped my life.
Time to preserve a legacy that deserves to live for generations.

This book is more than a collection of memories.
It is a tribute to a man whose heart made the world gentler.
It is a love letter from a daughter to her father.

It is a historical preservation of a family story that reaches deeply into the roots of South Texas — all the way to the Bruni and Henry lineage and even to early American history.

But more than anything, it is a testament to what kindness looks like when it becomes a lifestyle.

## What This Book Holds

Inside these pages, you will meet the man I was privileged to call my father:

- a boy shaped by humble beginnings
- a son of a resilient mother, Herlinda Bruni
- a grandson descended from the Bruni Mineral legacy
- a young man strengthened by responsibility
- a devoted husband
- a father with a heart as wide as Texas
- a protector, a provider, a peacemaker
- a gentleman in every quiet detail
- and finally, an angel watching over us from heaven

You will read about laughter, heartbreak, faith, adventure, and the stories that made us who we are. You will walk with us through his childhood, the loss of his son Jimmy, the beautiful bond with his siblings, and the joyful arrival of his granddaughter Lori — his Lullah Bella.

You will see how he built businesses, how he treated tenants with compassion, how he worked tirelessly, and how he carried an innocence and humor that softened everyone who knew him.

You will step with us into the sacredness of his final days — the moment heaven touched earth and angels arrived for him.

You will learn what legacy really means.

## Why I Chose to Share This Story

There are many men in this world, but few like my father. He lived without ego.

He spoke without judgment.
He gave without expecting anything in return.
He believed in kindness more than material success.
He chose grace over anger, patience over frustration, faith over fear.

In a world that is sometimes too loud, too fast, too harsh, I felt compelled to preserve the example of a man who moved through life gently — but left an impact that will echo for generations.

I wrote this book because:

- I want future generations to know him.
- I want my grandchildren to understand the legacy they come from.
- I want his story to be recorded as part of our family history.
- I want the world to remember that true greatness is found in humility, simplicity, and love.

This book is a memorial, a celebration, and a gift — not just to my family but to anyone who believes that a good heart can change the world.

## A Legacy Meant to Outlive Us All

My father built a legacy not through wealth but through humanity.
His influence can be seen in the real estate he developed, the trust he helped manage, the families he supported, the tenants he helped, the siblings he protected, the neighbors he uplifted, and the grandchildren he adored.

He left footprints on our hearts that no time can erase.

In writing this book, I am ensuring that:

- his story is preserved
- his sacrifices are remembered
- his humanity is honored
- his lessons are passed down
- and his unwavering love continues to guide us

Everychapter is a piece of him — the man, the father, the grandfather, and the angel he has become.

## From My Heart to Yours

As you begin this journey, I ask you to read these pages not just with your mind, but with your heart. Know that every sentence was written with love. Know that every memory carries the weight of gratitude. Know that every chapter is a gift I offer to the world — in honor of the man who gave me everything.

Now, with love, reverence, and courage...
I welcome you into his story.

The story of Ernesto Ramirez.
The man with the big heart.

The man I called Dad.

# Part I Lineage and Foundations

# Chapter 1
# Lineage of Strength
# The Bruni and Henry Legacy

✦✦✦ ═══ ✧ ═══ ✦✦✦

## A Legacy Few Knew About

Every family carries a history.
Some of it is lived.
Some of it is told.
Some of it — waits quietly in the soil, in the records, in the unspoken lineage of those who came before us.

While my father's early life shaped his heart... his deeper lineage held a story tied to land, history, leadership, and legacy — quietly connected to the foundations of South Texas and perhaps even the roots of the nation itself.

This part of his story wasn't widely discussed at family tables.
There were no boasts, no claims, no prideful conversations.

It was almost as if God preserved it quietly — waiting for the right generation to uncover it.

Maybe — this book is part of that unveiling.

## The Bruni Bloodline – A Heritage of Land, Leadership and Legacy

My father's mother, Herlinda Bruni Ramirez, was the daughter of Concelación Henry and Antonio Mateo Bruni (A.M. Bruni) — the very man whose name would become tied to history through the founding of:

- The Bruni Mineral Trust
- The town of Bruni, Texas
- A legacy of land, oil, gas, cattle, and uranium

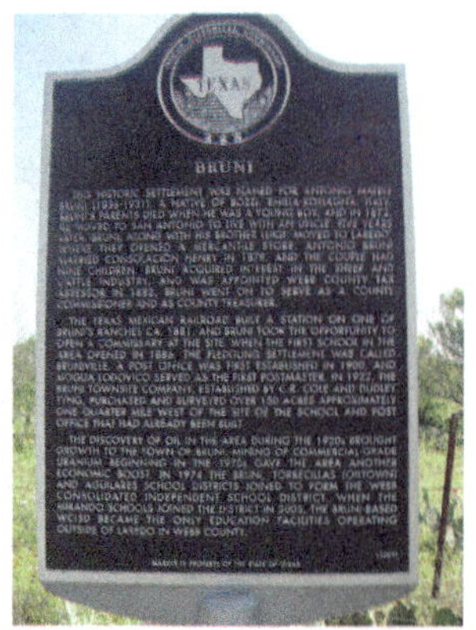


Though my father grew up humbly — without extravagance and never with entitlement — his lineage held remarkable roots.

His grandfather, A.M. Bruni was one of the early visionaries who helped shape the economic foundation of South Texas.

A historical marker, set by the Texas Historical Commission, tells his story clearly:

> "This historic settlement was named for Antonio
>
> Mateo Bruni (1856–1931),
> a native of Bozzi, Emilia-Romagna, Italy. Bruni's parents died when he was young, and in 1872 he moved to San Antonio to live with an uncle. Five years later, Bruni — along with his brother Luigi — moved to Laredo, where they opened a mercantile store.
>
> In 1879, Antonio Bruni married Concelación Henry, and together they had nine children.
>
> Bruni acquired interest in the sheep and cattle industry, served Webb County as tax assessor in 1882, and later as County Treasurer and County Commissioner."

As time passed, oil was discovered on his land.
Uranium was later found in the area in the 1970s, bringing economic growth and opportunity The Bruni Mineral Trust grew — not just as a family asset — but as a contributing force to the development of Webb County and South Texas education.

In 2005, the Bruni-based WCISD became the *only education facility operating outside of Laredo.*

Even in history... service to the community remained part of their DNA.

## The Henry Line — A Deeper American Thread

But the story goes even further.

Through Concelación Henry, family history points to an even deeper root — one that touches the story of America itself.

It is believed that through her lineage, we may trace our ancestry to Patrick Henry, one of the Founding Fathers of the United States — known for his powerful declaration during the American Revolution:

> ***"Give me liberty, or give me death!"***

Whether or not every line of lineage can be officially proven — the spirit of those words was alive in my father.

He lived his life with quiet conviction.
He stood for principle.
He believed in freedom, fairness, faith, and responsibility.
He never demanded attention — but always did what was right.

That is legacy.
Whether written in bloodlines — or written in character.

## A Humble Childhood – A Noble Heart

What makes his life so extraordinary is that he grew up without privilege, without the comfort of wealth — even though the seeds of legacy were already planted generations before him.

He was raised simply... and yet he lived nobly.

He learned values before he gained resources.
He learned kindness before he gained opportunity.
He learned resilience before he gained blessing.

This is why — when the mineral rights began to prosper — he did not change.

> He didn't use money to elevate himself.
> He used it to serve.
> To invest.
> To provide.
> To build a life for his family — one house at a time.

That is the greatest triumph of all:
He had access to privilege...
but never relied on it.

His legacy was not inherited —
It was chosen.
Day by day.
With character, work ethic, and generosity.

## What His Roots Reveal About Him

From one side of his story came struggle — and the courage to endure it.

From the other — came opportunity — and the humility to honor it.

Both sides shaped him.

Both sides built him.

Both sides lived within him.

From these roots, he learned:

- Responsibility — not as duty, but as love in action
- Resilience — born from challenges he never asked for
- Loyalty — because family wasn't optional; family was everything
- Faith — because sometimes, that was all they had to hold on to

Hardship built his strength.
History planted his heritage.
But his character — that came from the choices he made every day.

That is why his story matters.
Not just because of where he came from —
but because of who he chose to become.

## Reflections – Crossing Two Worlds Beautifully

He crossed two worlds beautifully:
The world of humble beginnings
and the world of historic lineage

But he never clung to either one.

He simply lived —
with gratitude,
with faith,
and with a quiet strength that required no applause.

His legacy is not held in history books...
It is held in our hearts.
In that quiet truth —
his life still speaks.

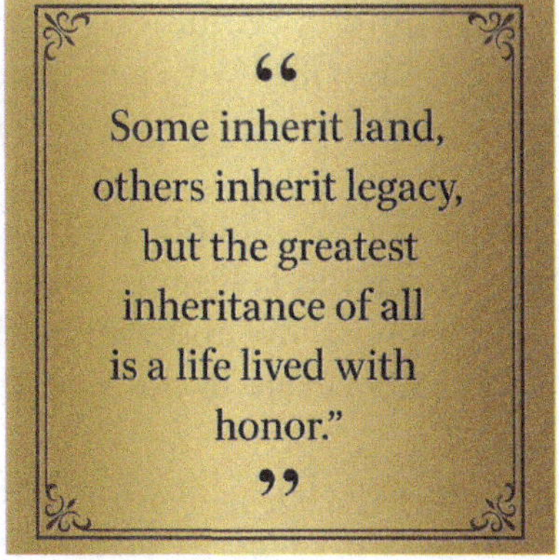

## Chapter 2
# Roots of Strength

✦✦✦ ═══ ✧ ═══ ✦✦✦

### A Family of Ten • A Mother Who Became Both Mom & Dad • Lessons from Humble Beginnings

Every great life story begins somewhere — not always with comfort, not always with ease, but often with a defining moment that shapes the heart long before anyone realizes its impact. My father, Ernesto Ramirez, came from humble beginnings. He was one of ten children, raised in a small, lively home filled with love, noise, shared meals, and the kind of unity that only hardship has the power to forge.

In this cherished photo are Lalo Benavides, his sister Gloria Benavides, their mother Herlinda Ramirez Bruni, and Alicia Ramirez — four pillars of the family whose love and strength helped shape the legacy of Ernesto Ramirez. Mom and dad are to the right after Alicia Ramirez.

Life did not start gently for my father.
It began with a test — one that would mold his strength, his patience, and his compassion for the rest of his life.

When he was still very young, his father left the family — walking away from a devoted wife and ten children who had depended on him.

In a world that already demanded more of women than anyone ever admitted, my grandmother suddenly carried the weight of both roles: mother and father, comforter and disciplinarian, nurturer and protector.

This moment could have broken their home.
Instead, it revealed its strength.

My grandmother stepped into her new reality with courage and grace. She did not crumble. She did not give in to despair. She did not allow bitterness to poison her spirit. Instead, she stood firm and steady for her children, teaching them not only to survive, but to persevere — to work hard, to love deeply, to rely on one another, and to trust that God never abandons His children.

Although life was difficult in countless ways, there were also moments of comfort woven into their childhood. As the children grew older, there were usually several housekeepers in the home — women who cooked, cleaned, and helped my grandmother with the enormous responsibility of raising ten children. Their home never lacked movement, laughter, or conversation. Every evening, without fail, there was a feast laid out on the table — warm, abundant meals prepared with love and care.

My dad would laugh every time he shared this memory.
Despite the abundance of food — the rice, beans, handmade tortillas, roasted meats, and desserts — he always wanted just one simple thing, the same thing every time:

"Mama, can I have a nickel to go buy a hamburger?"

Even with a full table in front of him, he longed for something small and familiar — that five-cent hamburger down the street that made him feel free and happy.

My grandmother would shake her head, smiling, because she knew him so well. While Papu (my dad) walked down the street to get his little hamburger, Aunt Gloria and the rest of the sisters stayed behind to enjoy the feast, laughing together, sharing stories, and savoring the warm meals placed lovingly before them.

I always remembered my mother telling this story with such affection — how the girls stayed home to enjoy the feast while my father followed his heart straight to that simple hamburger. The memory became a cherished reminder of who he was even as a boy: joyful, independent, easy to please, and drawn to the simple things.

Years later, the lesson in that story became clear:

Even when life offered plenty...
Even when the table was full...
He cherished the small things — the little joys, the familiar comforts, the modest blessings.

From those early years, he carried a truth that shaped his entire life:

Happiness is not found in luxury.
Happiness is found in simplicity, gratitude, and knowing what truly matters.

My father's life was a perfect reflection of this truth. Even as he grew older, he never chased after wealth or extravagance. He found joy in the most ordinary things — things that would go unnoticed by many, but meant everything to him.

As a young man, his brother gave him an old truck. Most people might have seen it as just a vehicle past its prime, but to Dad, it was a treasure. He drove that truck with pride, and it became part of his daily life for nearly twenty years. It didn't matter that it wasn't new or fancy — it worked, it carried him where he needed to go, and that was enough.

He didn't measure life by the shine of material things.
He measured it by purpose, usefulness, and gratitude.

His simplicity extended to everything, even his clothing. He dressed with modesty and humility, choosing what was comfortable and practical. He never tried to impress anyone, never dressed beyond his means, and never felt the need to keep up with anyone else's standards. His contentment came from knowing who he was, not from what he wore.

That was one of the most beautiful things about him —
his ability to remain grounded in a world that often confuses luxury with value.

To him, a dependable old truck, a clean shirt, and a grateful heart were far more meaningful than anything money could buy. His life was a quiet reminder that simplicity is not a limitation — it is a blessing, a choice, and a pathway to peace.

From this foundation came my father's quiet strength — the kind of strength that never demanded attention, never needed to be explained, and never sought praise. It simply existed, steady and faithful as the sunrise. He learned firsthand that family is not defined by who stays during the easy seasons, but by who stands tall when life becomes hard.

He learned that true leadership isn't loud — it is revealed through action:

- in showing up,
- in protecting,
- in providing,
- in sacrificing,
- in doing what must be done with a humble heart.

These beginnings did not weaken him — they forged him.

They taught him to cherish family, to find joy in simple things, and to face the world with quiet courage and steady hands. His childhood shaped every part of who he would later become: the loving father, the devoted husband, the treasured grandfather, the dependable brother, and the unforgettable friend.

To the world, it may have looked like a story of struggle — an abandoned wife and ten children trying to survive.

But what God saw was something very different:
The birth of strength, unity, and divine purpose.

What looked like loss became a school of perseverance.
What looked like hardship became a lesson in faith.

No one could've predicted that from this humble home would raise a man with a heart so big, so joyful, so giving, that everyone who crossed his path felt richer because of him.

He grew up with everything that mattered — love, faith, unity, laughter, and the unbreakable bond of a mother who refused to surrender.

These lessons — born from sacrifice and steadied by prayer — became the roots that anchored his soul. They held him firm through every storm and gave him the strength to build a life overflowing with generosity, humor, kindness, and love.

He gave his children and a grandchild something priceless:
a legacy of love, laughter, and unshakable family strength.

In his home, under the protection of a resilient woman who refused to give up, God planted something powerful — a family that learned to endure, to rise, and to love deeply.

> "Her children rise up and call her blessed." — Proverbs 31:28

Through all her sacrifices, God revealed another truth:

> "Train up a child in the way he should go; and when he is old,
> he will not depart from it." — Proverbs 22:6

This was the beginning of his story —a story strengthened by faith, shaped by family, and lifted by the grace of God.

## Chapter 3

# The Boy Who Became a Gentle Giant

✦✦✦ ══════ ◇ ══════ ✦✦✦

### Childhood Values • Faith • Work Ethic • Responsibility • A Heart Shaped by Life's Trials

A gentle heart is rarely born out of easy days.
It is formed through struggle, strengthened through love, and polished through responsibility.

From the beginning, Ernesto Ramirez grew up in a world where family was everything. Ten children under one roof meant laughter and chaos, sharing and sacrifice, and a sense of belonging that many families never know. But what shaped him most wasn't the size of the family — it was the weight of responsibility each child learned to carry.

## A Childhood Built on Responsibility

With ten children, there was no room for laziness and no time for selfishness. Every child was needed. Every child contributed. That truth planted in Ernesto a deep understanding of work, duty, loyalty, and discipline.

In a family that large, everyone stepped in.

The older children learned to drive before the younger ones, so they could help the family — running errands, picking up necessities, delivering messages, or helping their mother however she needed. They learned to work as a team, to rely on each other, and to act quickly when the household needed something done.

Those early experiences shaped Ernesto's character deeply. He learned:

- To pay attention when others needed help
- To step forward without waiting to be asked
- To do things with pride, not complaint
- To understand the value of contributing to something bigger than himself

Thesewere the seeds of responsibility that later grew into his work ethic, his reliability, and his reputation as a man who could always be counted on.

## A Childhood Interrupted by Asthma

Although he was strong in spirit, young Ernesto's body often struggled. From an early age, he suffered from severe asthma — the kind that would come suddenly, take his breath away, and turn even a quiet afternoon into a moment of fear. My mother would tell me stories of how he would sometimes run out of the house, gasping for air, desperate to breathe, desperate to find relief. Those moments were terrifying for a little boy, especially one with such a tender heart.

His brothers and sisters helped him with schoolwork, explained lessons, cared for him when he was sick, and made sure he never felt alone or discouraged. Their tenderness shaped him just as much as his mother's strength did.

Asthma taught him patience.
His siblings taught him compassion.
Together, those moments taught him humility.

This is why, later in life, Ernesto never judged anyone, never rushed anyone, and never looked down on anyone struggling. He knew what it was like to need help — and he never forgot it.

## Learning to Work — The Ramirez Way

As he grew into his teenage years, Ernesto began learning not only responsibility, but opportunity. His father, Mr. Ramirez, owned the DeSoto Car Dealership, and that dealership marked the beginning of Ernesto's career.

It was not glamorous work.
It wasn't easy work.
But it was honest work — and he loved it.

Side by side with his brothers, he learned and understood the family business. Being at the dealership meant more than earning money; it meant learning:

- How to speak respectfully to adults
- How to look people in the eye
- How to show up on time
- How to work even when tired
- How to keep going even when life demanded more than he had

While many boys his age were wasting time, Ernesto was developing habits that would follow him for the rest of his life.

## The Job That Changed Everything — KGNS Television

From the dealership, Ernesto transitioned to a job that would shape him for decades — working at the local television station, the one we know today as KGNS.

Back then, it went by another name.
But for him, it wasn't about the name — it was about the opportunity.

He worked there for many years, becoming a familiar face, a trusted worker, and a man who treated every task with seriousness and pride. He learned the rhythm of the station — the cameras, the equipment, the hum of production behind the scenes. He spliced film reels, prepared segments for shows and commercials, and handled a little bit of everything that needed to be done. While not every technical detail is remembered today, one thing is certain: my dad approached every responsibility as if he were running the station himself.

He did that because he truly grew to love his work. The station became more than a workplace — it became a part of his identity, a place where his dedication meant something, and where he poured his heart into every task. His passion became so strong that he eventually brought my brother into KGNS as well. Seeing my dad's devotion inspired my brother to follow in his footsteps. My brother later went off to study to become a television technician. Back then, TV stations didn't simply "turn on" — someone had to travel miles, climb to the broadcasting site, and activate the switch that brought television to life each morning. My brother became that person, the one ensuring the signal went out, carrying forward the legacy that my father had quietly started.

In that simple, humble way, my father passed down more than a job — he passed down passion, responsibility, and pride in one's work.

## Summers in the Sun – Delivering Mail

During the summers, Ernesto added another job to his list: working for the postal service. He delivered mail, walked routes in the heat, and learned another level of discipline.

The postal service taught him:

- Endurance
- Consistency
- Accountability
- And the importance of serving the community

He worked hard, showed up faithfully, and carried himself with integrity in everything he did.

## Real Estate: The Quiet Entrepreneur With a Servant's Heart

As Ernesto grew into adulthood, another side of him began to emerge — the entrepreneur. My dad didn't announce it, boast about it, or chase wealth. Instead, he began building his future the same way he approached everything else in life: slowly, humbly, and with an incredible work ethic.

He entered the world of real estate, starting with small rental homes and gradually expanding to duplexes, apartment units, and even a few houses. Every property he owned, he cared for with his own hands. He was not the kind of landlord who hired people to repair, clean, or maintain his buildings — he became all of those things himself.

My dad painted walls, cleaned apartments, fixed toilets, repaired faucets, handled small plumbing issues, and took care of the lawns and exterior work. If a tenant moved out, he was the one sweeping, scrubbing, repainting, and preparing the home for the next family. He didn't just manage properties — he nurtured them.

He approached real estate the same way he approached life: responsibly, steadily, and from the heart.

He would buy one property, pay it off with discipline, and then move on to the next. Over time, this simple, consistent approach grew into what became E&A Ramirez Rentals, a partnership built on trust, devotion, and years of hard work.

But what truly set him apart was not his business sense — it was his kindness.

When tenants struggled to pay their rent, he never scolded, threatened, or pressured them. He would simply knock on the door and gently ask:

"¿Dónde está la renta?"

If they said, "I'm sorry, Mr. Ramirez... I don't have it today."
He would nod kindly and say:

"Está bien. Just let me know when you can."

Weeks might go by.
He would still wait — patiently, quietly, wholeheartedly.

My mother would tease him, asking:

"Ernesto, are you running a business or a charity?"

But that was who he was.
He believed people deserved understanding.
He believed dignity mattered.
He believed compassion was more important than money.

In real estate, as in everything else, my dad's heart was always bigger than the job.

## The Making of a Gentle Giant

From the outside, these might look like simple childhood and young adult experiences. But for my dad, they were the building blocks of a life shaped by responsibility, humility, and quiet strength.

He wasn't loud.
He wasn't boastful.
He wasn't the kind of man who needed attention.

He was the boy who grew up learning responsibility through family, empathy through illness, discipline through work, and purpose through service.

These years carved the foundation of who he would become:

- A man of a big heart
- A man of gentle humor
- A man whose innocence remained untouched
- A man who worked hard without complaint
- A man who loved deeply without conditions

He learned that strength isn't about muscles or pride or domination. Strength is about showing up — day after day, year after year — for the people who need you.

He learned that responsibility is not just a burden; it is an honor.

He learned that a good man is not defined by what he has, but by who he is when no one is watching.

## A Gentle Heart Forged by Life

By the time Ernesto reached adulthood, he was not hardened by life — he was softened by it. His trials made him patient. His illnesses made him tender. His family made him loyal. His jobs made him dependable. Everything he touched was done with care. Everything he loved, he loved with his whole heart.

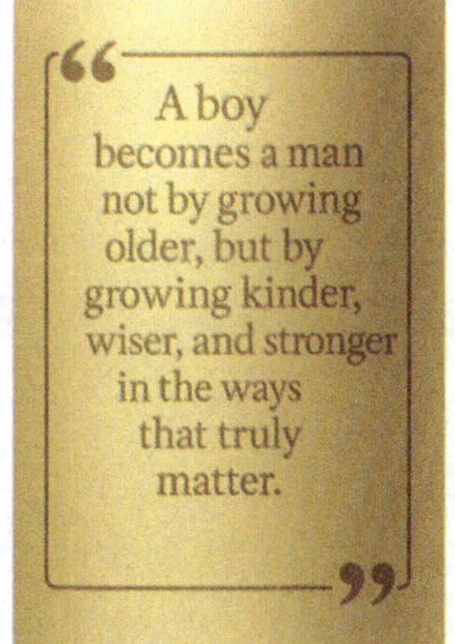


Everything he endured, he endured with grace.

This is how a boy became a gentle giant. Not through ease — but through life, love, hardship, and gratitude.

# Part II

# The Man He Became

# Chapter 4
# Protector of Hearts

## Love in Action, Courage in Silence

A protector is not always the loudest person in the room. Sometimes, the greatest protectors are quiet souls who watch over everyone with tender eyes and a steady heart. My father was that kind of protector — calm, humble, watchful, and ready to act in an instant.

He did not need to raise his voice or use force to prove his strength. Instead, his love was his strength. His presence felt like safety — a blanket of peace that wrapped around you without a word. With him near, you knew everything would be alright. Always.

He had a gentle nature, but underneath it lived a fierce commitment: Family first. Always. He lived by that promise — not in speeches but in quiet actions. Quiet actions, I've learned, are the truest form of love there is.

## The Day He Jumped In

One of the earliest memories that reveals who he truly was happened by a swimming pool. I was just a little girl — full of excitement, curiosity, and absolutely no sense of danger. When I saw the sparkling water, I didn't think twice — I jumped right in.

There was only one problem:
I didn't know how to swim.

In that split second, panic should have filled the air. But instead, there was only swift movement — instinctive, certain, fueled by love.

Without hesitation or fear, my father dove in after me.
There were no dramatic pauses, no calculations, no questions. His baby was in trouble — and that was enough.

He pulled me out of the water as effortlessly as breathing. In that moment, even before I knew what love was, I understood that love jumps.

Love leaps.
Love rescues.

He didn't need to tell me he would always protect me.
He showed me.

## Safety Was His Language of Love

He wasn't a man who talked endlessly about defending his family — **he simply did it.** Quietly. Consistently. Faithfully.

He stood between us and worried.
He stood between us and fear.
He stood between us and the world when it felt too big, too loud, or too heavy.

Yet, he never smothered us. He never controlled us.
He simply made sure that when life felt like deep waters...
**We always had a hand to hold.**

It wasn't just physical protection he offered.
It was **emotional safety.**
**Spiritual safety.**
**Soul safety.**

His love was a shield we didn't fully recognize until we grew up — and then realized how rare such protection truly is.

## Protecting With Heart, Not Hardness

Many believe protection requires harshness.
But **his protection was tenderness.**

He didn't intimidate.
He didn't threaten.
He never needed to be harsh to be strong.

Instead, he protected us with:

- Warmth
- Gentleness
- Steadiness
- Presence

He showed us that **love didn't need to be loud to be powerful** — and strength did not need to be forceful to be real. That kind of protection stays long after someone is gone.

Even now, when life feels uncertain, I can still feel that blanket of safety around me — the one made from his love.

His protection did not end.
**It simply changed form.**

## A Protector of People and Animals

His protective heart extended far beyond his family. He had a compassion that instinctively reached toward anyone — *or anything* — in need.

One afternoon while working as a trustee at the **Bruni Mineral Trust,** he went outside to dispose of some trash. As he walked toward the dumpster, he heard something — small... faint... that was crying. Curious, he looked inside and found **four tiny kittens,** shivering and abandoned.

## A Work Ethic That Shaped a Gentleman

One of the most meaningful responsibilities my father ever carried was his role with the **Bruni Mineral Trust** — an oil and gas mineral rights entity that managed approximately **160,000 acres across Webb and surrounding counties.**

Most people would have seen that role as business.
But to him — it was **family, heritage,** and **duty with purpose.**

He sought out that position with humility and respect.
When he was elected to serve as a trustee, he treated it like a sacred responsibility — one passed down through generations.

For **25 years**, he served as Trustee, quietly shaping the future of lands and families. In his early years, everything was handled the old-fashioned way: checks were **mailed to the post office**, documents were carefully reviewed by hand, and my dad — always dependable — would collect those checks and personally take them to different banks for deposit.

It wasn't glamorous.
It wasn't quick.
But he approached every step with precision, integrity, and pride.

He believed that when someone trusts you with responsibility — you honor that trust with excellence.

Most would have walked away.
But not him.

He **jumped into the dumpster**, rescued all four kittens, and carefully brought them home. My mother asked, "Ernesto, what is this?"
He replied simply —
*"I couldn't leave them there."*

They kept the kittens. One of them grew sick and developed cancer in his paw — but Dad made sure he received treatment, medication, and love. He never saw stray animals as a burden. To him, they were souls who needed care.

Another time, while visiting my brother Jimmy at the cemetery, he heard another cry — from inside the bushes. He searched — and found another kitten, alone and scared. As always, he picked it up, brought it home, and told my mother:
*"How could I leave him alone at the cemetery? He had to come home with me."*

He was a guardian — not just of people, but of anything that needed protection. Even the smallest, quietest creatures were safe when he was around.

In those small, humble acts... **his heart spoke louder than words ever could.**

## Quiet Courage, Noble Strength

Heroes don't always wear capes.
Sometimes they wear kindness.
Sometimes they wear patience.
Sometimes they wear a simple, humble smile.

My father didn't go around declaring his bravery —
**he just lived it.**

He jumped into pools.
He stepped into storms.
He rescued kittens from dumpsters and cemeteries.
He offered help when no one asked.

He gave when no one expected.
And he loved when the world was unkind.

His courage was steady, consistent, and quiet.
It stood in silence —
but **it stood strong.**

## A Protector Sent by God

I truly believe that God places certain souls on this earth not only to love us — but to protect us in ways we may never fully understand. My father was one of those souls.

He didn't just protect our safety.
He protected our hearts.

That kind of protection doesn't fade when a person leaves this earth. It becomes spiritual. Eternal. It becomes part of who we are. When God places a protector in your life, that role doesn't vanish. It transforms. What began on earth continues from heaven, steady and faithful as ever.

## Reflection – Seeing Life Through a Big Heart

When we look at the life of a man like Ernesto Ramirez, we are reminded that greatness is not always loud... not always dramatic... not always on display.

Sometimes greatness is quiet:

- A hand reaching out without being asked.
- A gentle laugh that lightens the room.
- A willingness to rescue a kitten... or a child.
- A heart that sees the good in people — even when the world does not.

He protected — not because it was his duty — but because it was his nature. He didn't analyze kindness. He simply was kind.
He didn't calculate love. He simply loved.

When someone with a heart like his passes through your life, they leave you different — softer, wiser, more aware of the beauty in everyday moments.

His life reminds us that every small act of goodness ripples far beyond the moment it happens.

A gentle man can shape generations.
A big heart can become a legacy.

**Closing Thought**

> *"Some protect with their strength.*
>
> *The rare ones protect with their love.*
>
> *Those are the guardians heaven sends to earth."*

# Chapter 5

# Adventures andTravels

✦✦✦ ✧ ✦✦✦

## He Gave Us the World, One Memory at a Time

Some fathers bring home gifts.
Mine brought home experiences — moments so rich and joyful they still live in my heart as if they happened yesterday.

My father believed the world was meant to be explored, savored, and celebrated. He carried a quiet conviction that life was a treasure chest, and every journey held something golden inside it — laughter, wonder, curiosity, and togetherness. He didn't believe in standing still. He believed in discovering life, and he took us with him every step of the way.

From cruises to Disney magic, from Mexico to the Gulf Coast, he made sure our lives were filled with movement, discovery, and memories we would carry for a lifetime. Looking back, I realize something powerful:
He didn't just take us places — he showed us what it felt like to truly live.

## Our Disney Days — Where Magic Became Reality

Disneyland. Disney World. The happiest places on earth.

To my father, they weren't just amusement parks — they were playgrounds for the soul. He believed in the magic there, in the joy on every child's face, in the music, the colors, the parades, and the sense of possibility floating in the air.

We would ride It's a Small World again and again — not because the ride changed, but because we did, each time filling our hearts a little more with wonder. He watched us more than the rides. He looked at our faces when we laughed. He was the kind of father who saw his joy reflected in ours.

At night, exhausted from walking,eating, laughing, and chasing dreams, I would tell him,

"Dad, not too early tomorrow. We need to rest."

He would smile sweetly and promise he wouldn't wake us too soon.

Then, without fail, a gentle knock would come at the door by 8 or 9 a.m.: "Are you all up yet, honey?"

There was never pressure. Never rush. Just love, excitement, and possibility — a new day waiting to be written.

That was how he woke us up — softly, patiently, lovingly. Not with urgency... but with hope.

Those mornings were never just mornings.
They were invitations to live another beautiful day — together.

## Cruises, Calm Seas and Life's Unexpected Storms

As a young girl, some of my favorite memories with my parents were the many cruises we took together. One of the ships we sailed on several times was the SS Norway — a magnificent blue vessel that felt like a floating world of excitement, adventure, and endless possibility.

I remember the thrill of boarding, the sound of the horn echoing across the port, and the way my father's eyes lit up every single time as if he were stepping into a brand-new discovery. There was something about a cruise ship that made him feel alive. The sea, the music, the shows, the food — all of it awakened a joy inside of him that was contagious.

We weren't wealthy.
We didn't travel for luxury.
We traveled for life.

Later on, my parents even went on a Disney cruise, and the childlike excitement never faded. Dad loved anything magical — anything that allowed him to explore, experience, or laugh. That was his heart: always open, always adventurous, always full.

I can still see him leaning over the ship's railing, staring into the ocean with a peace that felt holy. Sometimes he didn't say much. He didn't have to. His joy was evident in the way he looked at the sunrise, at the laughter around him, at the people he loved.

I think that's why I cherish those memories —not because of the ocean but because of who I saw when I looked at him.

## The Hurricane That Couldn't Shake Him

One year, a hurricane passed through the Gulf as we were flying home from a cruise. The turbulence was rough, and by the time we landed in Houston, every flight had been grounded. We were stranded — tired, confused, and unsure of what to do next.

But not once did my father panic.
Not once did he complain.
Not once did fear touch his voice.

Instead, he guided us through the chaos as if it were part of the adventure. He found a hotel, made sure we all had dinner, kept our spirits light, and reassured us that everything would be fine — because with him, it always was.

Dad had a remarkable gift:
When he stayed calm, everyone else did, too.

Even in unexpected storms — whether in life or on the way home from vacation — he made everything feel safe. Even the uncertainties felt lighter when he was there. His quiet confidence didn't just carry him — it carried us all.

Now, looking back, I understand what those moments meant.
Adventure wasn't about the destination.
It was about the person we were with.

## He Taught Us What Real Adventure Means

Traveling with my dad wasn't about luxury or showing off. It was about appreciation. About value. About time. He taught us that memory mattered more than money, that together was the best destination, and that joy could be found anywhere — if you carried the right heart with you.

He showed us that the world is beautiful not because of the places on a map...but because of the people we share it with.

He showed us that adventure could look like:

✓ Riding It's a Small World ten times
✓ Squeezing into a tiny hotel room with laughter
✓ Eating simple meals while sharing stories
✓ Watching parades with wide eyes
✓ Standing calmly in the middle of a crisis

Adventure wasn't defined by where we went, it was defined by who we were with.

## Reflection — His Heart Was the Real Destination

Now I know the truth:
The greatest journey wasn't to Disney or Mexico or the ocean.
The greatest journey was walking beside my father —

On every sidewalk, every ship deck, every sunrise...
He was the adventure.

It wasn't about where we went.
It was about who we became because of him.

He gave me more than memories.
He gave me courage.
He gave me faith.
He gave me a heart that believes the world is good.

Even now...
when I close my eyes and hear a cruise ship horn,
or laughter on a theme park ride,
or the softest morning knock at my door...
I still feel him there.

> **The best places we ever traveled weren't found on a map—they were found in the moments when we laughed together, forgot our worries, and simply lived with grateful hearts.**
>
> Inspired by the journeys of Ernesto Ramirez, who explored the world not just with his feet, but with a big, beautiful heart.

# Chapter 6
# Beyond the Map Finding Joy Everywhere We Went

✦✦✦ ══════ ✧ ══════ ✦✦✦

## Family, Friendship and Finding Joy Everywhere

While Disney and cruise ships gave us magic — the road trips across Mexico gave us stories, lessons, and laughter that shaped our hearts forever.

Those journeys were not just vacations. They were classrooms. They were windows into culture, into courage, into human kindness — and into how a man with a big heart led with joy rather than fear. My father believed that every trip had a purpose, and every person we met had something to teach us. That's why he loved Mexico so much — not just because it was beautiful but because it was alive.

## Monterrey and Saltillo: The Road That Taught Us Courage

One of our earliest adventures took us across the border to Monterrey and then into the stunning town of Saltillo. We traveled as one big family group — my parents, Aunt Gloria, several of her children, and me — in two Suburbans packed with luggage, snacks, excitement, and more joy than space.

Two matching vehicles driving in line across Mexico?
Of course, that caught attention.

Somewhere along the road into Monterrey, police waved us over. Not because we did anything wrong — but because in those days, traveling caravans were always questioned. My father remained calm as the officers approached. They quickly realized we were American families on vacation, and like many travelers at that time understood, a mordida — a harmless bribe — was expected. With a smile and a respectful gesture, my father handled it with grace. No fear. No fuss. Just part of the journey.

That was the first moment I realized something important:
It wasn't the obstacles that mattered — it was how you responded to them.

The road continued, and soon the mountains rose before us like guardians welcoming us home. In Saltillo, the air felt fresher, the sunsets felt softer, and laughter somehow felt louder. My father took us to scenic spots, historic plazas, and places where time seemed to slow down. The weather was perfect — cool but bright — and everywhere we looked, beauty waited to be seen.

Saltillo became one of those places that stayed in your heart long after you left it. We didn't have luxury, but we had something better — wonder. My father showed us that joy was not found in fancy hotels — but in shared meals, laughter, discovery, and the simple feeling of being safe with family.

## Mexico City — Squeezed Into a Beetle and Full of Laughter

Mexico City felt like another world. It was colorful, loud, historic, and full of culture and energy. One night after a celebration, we wandered the streets laughing and looking for a taxi — but none were in sight. Then, like a little miracle, a tiny Volkswagen Beetle pulled up.

The driver said:
"Solo cuatro pasajeros."
Only four passengers.

We insisted:
"Hay espacio para todos."
There's space for everyone.

Before we knew it, that little Beetle was filled with far more than four passengers — and ten hearts beating with joy. Every inch of that tiny car carried laughter. To this day, we still wonder how we all fit. But somehow... we did.

That ride became a metaphor for life:
Sometimes what looks too small... fits perfectly because love makes room.

## Acapulco, Cantinflas and The Surprise You Can't Plan

Another unforgettable trip took us to Acapulco — a place full of sun, music, and life. That trip became extra special when my mother — standing in a hotel lobby — noticed a familiar face. She approached him carefully and asked:

"¿Usted es Cantinflas...?"

CANTINFLAS

He turned with a big smile. It truly was him.
She was thrilled. We were all amazed. And for a moment — we were standing inside our own movie.

Life has magical moments that cannot be scheduled — they simply show up... when you're paying attention.

## Mexico City and Acapulco with The Valls Family

### *The Adventure That Strengthened Our Bonds*

Not all trips were just family — some were friendship woven into memories. Another beautiful vacation was spent with our neighbors and dear friends, Mr. Alfonso Valls and his family. Together, we traveled to Mexico City and Acapulco and stayed at the Princess Hotel, a place that would forever stay in our hearts.

It wasn't the kind of luxury that impressed people. It was the kind of joy that changed people. I still remember the boys — Pat, Kenny, and Mark — along with me, getting the chance to go parasailing for the first time.

We were so thin and light as kids that the instructors had to add extra weight to our parasails. They smiled and said,
"We need to help you fly."

Sometimes... life just needs a little extra push to lift you higher.

That moment became a lesson:
Fear and excitement often live in the same moment —
and courage is what turns fear into memory.

## Las Vegas — The Night Dad Walked Without Socks

Our trip to Las Vegas was filled with sparkle, wonder, and adventure — but like always, our father remained the gentle guide. He didn't gamble. He didn't seek to impress. He simply walked with us and made sure we were safe.

One night, my mother and I were downstairs in the casino, totally absorbed in playing the machines. Suddenly, Mom pointed in shock:

"Oh my God — there's a man coming with no socks!"
We looked up — and there he was.
Dad. Bare ankles and all. Walking across the casino floor, calm but firm.

"Do you know what time it is? It's 2 in the morning.
You two need to go back to your room!"

We burst out laughing. Not because he was scolding —
but because even his concern came wrapped in love and humor.

That night, I realized something:
Even his worried moments were delivered with kindness.
There was no anger. No judgment.
Only care. Only love.

## Teaching Us That Life Was Beautiful

Through every journey... he taught us how to live. He showed us:

- That the world was worth seeing
- That joy could be found anywhere —in a cruise ship... in a carnival... in a tiny Mexican taxi... or right at home.
- That memories meant more than things That family wasn't measured by blood — but by who you made room for in your heart and in your car
- That fear might visit — but joy should stay

He didn't raise his voice.
He didn't lead with pressure.
He led with kindness.
He left behind a life that proved:
Gentleness is a form of power.

## Reflection — What These Journeys Really Meant

As I look back, I see more than places.
I see lessons. I see values. I see the blueprint of a life well lived.

> "The best journeys are not measured in miles - but in the people we love enough to take with us."

My father didn't just teach us to travel.
He taught us to appreciate people.
To welcome strangers.
To see beauty everywhere.
To share joy.
To stay calm in fear.
To live with an open heart.
He didn't just show us the world.
He showed us how to live in it.

How to find joy everywhere you go.
How to welcome others in — even when there's only one seat left.

## Chapter 7

# When Hearts Break Losing Jimmy, Finding Strength Again

## Grief, Love, and the Strength of a Father's Heart

There are moments in life that divide time into "before" and "after." Moments so painful that the world seems to hold its breath and nothing feels the same.

For our family, one of those defining moments came when we lost Jimmy. He was so young — only 27 when he suffered a massive heart attack. Through God's grace and the strength within him, he lived five more years. But eventually, an aneurysm took him suddenly, leaving all of us heartbroken.

Jimmy was full of life — talented, funny, bright, and bursting with dreams. His presence lit up every room he entered, and his absence left a space that could never truly be filled.

He was a son, a brother, a friend... and a piece of our hearts.

When the news first came that he had suffered a massive heart attack, time froze
Fear settled in.
Hope fought back.
Prayer filled every breath.

Through it all, my father — so strong in his quiet way — held us together with tenderness, steadiness, and faith.

## The Fight for Life

They rushed to save him, but his condition was grave.
I still remember the doctor — compassion in his voice, weight in his eyes — saying:

"There's not much more we can do here."

But my parents were not ready to let go.
Love refuses to surrender easily.
A father's heart does not give up on his child.

When the specialist in San Antonio offered hope, however small... they took it. A military helicopter came — powerful, loud, urgent — and lifted Jimmy toward another chance at life.

My mother flew with him.
My father and I followed by car, carrying prayers in our chests and courage in our silence.

He lived five more years.
Five years gifted by grace, by love, by faith, and by the fierce devotion of a family who refused to stop believing.

When God finally called him home, the world felt different — quieter, heavier, changed.

## When Loss Meets Love

After Jimmy passed, something shifted in my parents — in my father, especially. Grief is not loud.
Sometimes it sits quietly in a chair.
Sometimes it stands outside on the porch
when the sun sets.

Sometimes it looks like silence... like a deep
breath held just a moment too long.
But even in heartbreak, his love did not break.
Even in sorrow, he stayed tender.
Even when his heart was aching,
he still reached for ours.
That's who he was — a man who carried
pain with dignity and still chose love every day.

The world did not take his kindness away.
It deepened it.

## His Passion That Kept Him Going: Jimmy and His Cars

One of the things that kept Jimmy going — even in the middle of his struggles — was his passion for cars. He didn't just like cars... he lived for them. They were his joy, his excitement, his escape, and one of the purest reflections of his personality.
I still remember the car he always dreamed of owning:
a Bricklin.

Back in the day, the Bricklin was something special — futuristic, unique, and unforgettable.
It had those iconic gull-wing doors that opened upward toward the sky with the push of a button. Jimmy loved everything about it. Because my parents were always willing to support his dreams, they searched for one until they finally found it in California.

They flew out to pick it up, and then drove it all the way back home — a trip filled with excitement and pride. That Bricklin meant everything to him.

But it didn't stop there.

Jimmy also owned a Pantera, Corvettes, and a Mustang through the years. Each one was a piece of his spirit — bold, bright, full of life. I remember how he talked about his cars, how he cared for them, and how they always seemed to bring out the spark in him.

Even years later, that spark still touches us.

Not long ago, I walked into Sames Motor Dealership and saw a Mustang sitting there on the floor. The moment I laid eyes on it, something in me stirred. It felt familiar... warm... like Jimmy was standing right beside me.

Without hesitation, I bought a Mustang convertible — the car that reminded me of him the most.

When I sat inside it for the first time, I felt his presence so strongly that the only words that came out were:

"Jimmy... this is for you."

It was my way of honoring him.
Of keeping a part of him alive.
Of holding onto the joy he carried everywhere he went.

Jimmy loved his cars — and now, his love for them lives on in me.

## The Light That Helped My Dad Stand Again

When Lori was born, joy returned like a sunrise after a long night.
Her little hands, her soft breaths, her innocent eyes — they healed places time alone could not reach.

She did not replace what was lost.
Nothing ever could.

But she brought purpose back into his mornings and laughter back into his evenings. He held her, fed her, rocked her, and whispered to her as if she were sent by heaven itself.

In truth, she was.

God gives comfort in the form of people — and she was comfort wrapped in love.

## Strength in Stillness

Some men show strength through words.
Some show it through power.
My father showed it through endurance, through faith, through the way he kept loving even when his heart was shattered.

He never blamed God.
He never let bitterness touch him.
He never stopped being gentle.
He never stopped being him.

He walked through the valley of grief with humility, faith, and grace — and he showed us that strength is not the absence of tears...strength is loving through them.

# Chapter 8
# Sisters and Soulmates
# His Lifelong Companions

## Bound by Blood, Strengthened by Love

Family is not just where we come from —it is where our hearts learn how to love, how to forgive, and how to stay connected through every season life brings.

For my father, family was sacred.
He came from a big family — ten children total, each one shaped by the same humble beginnings, the same lessons in strength and perseverance, and the same fierce loyalty to one another.

His childhood wasn't easy, yet somehow it produced hearts that were unbreakable in love and unwavering in devotion.

In that busy household, full of voices, hopes, and shared responsibility, Dad learned something priceless:

When life gives you siblings, it gives you forever.

## A Special Bond With His Sisters

Among his siblings, his bond with his sisters was something extraordinary — tender, joyful, constant.

Those girls weren't just his sisters.
They were his confidants.
His cheerleaders.
His lifelong companions.
His built-in circle of love.

He adored them —
every one of them —
and would have done anything for them.

They adored him back.

He had a special bond with one in particular — his sister Gloria.

They were, as many would say, "two peas in a pod".
In laughter and in tears, in childhood and adulthood, through sickness and celebration, they walked through life side by side.

Their connection was pure, steady, and rooted in an unspoken promise:
We take care of each other. Always.

## Childhood Roots That Followed Them Into Life

Growing up in a home where their mother became both mom and dad, each child played a part in keeping the family strong.

They learned to depend on one another, to uplift one another, to sacrifice when needed, and to stand together when the world felt uncertain.

Those early lessons in unity didn't stay in childhood — they traveled with him into adult life.

Vacations together, family gatherings, trips to the beach, shared laughter, and whispered conversations across decades — they didn't just survive as siblings, they thrived as soul-family.

When they went to the beach, it wasn't just a trip — it was belonging.
When they gathered, it wasn't just a meal — it was home.
When one needed help, the others arrived — no questions asked.

Family wasn't duty.
It was joy.
It was legacy.
It was love lived out loud.

Through Sickness and Through Celebration

Life tested them — like it tests all families.
There were moments of worry, moments of heartbreak, and seasons where illness tried to steal strength away from those they loved.

But Dad never left their side.
Just as they never left his.

When his sisters needed support, he showed up.
When they celebrated, he smiled the biggest.
When they hurt, he felt it in his own heart.

Love like that is rare —
but he carried it effortlessly, naturally, faithfully.

He didn't just have sisters —
he had angels he grew up with,
friends embedded deep in his soul,
and companions who walked beside him through life's journey.

## The Family You Choose

In every family story, there are people who don't share our blood — but somehow become part of our heart.

For us, that person was Lupita.

She came into our lives over forty years ago, when she began helping our family in the home. But very quickly, it became clear — she was never just the "help". From the moment she arrived, my parents treated her the way they treated everyone in their life — with respect, dignity, and love. Before long, she became part of us. She was not hired to help — she was *family.*

My father adored Lupita, and she adored him. She was there in the joyful times, and especially during the hardest ones. When she lost her mother and father, my dad stepped in and told her gently, *"Don't worry — I'll help you with the expenses. You're not alone. You have us."*

Because of my parents, Lupita was able to gain amnesty and become an American citizen — a life-changing opportunity she never forgot. To her, my parents were angels; and to us, she became a sister. I have always told her, "Mi casa es tu casa — my house is your house." I meant it.

We all did.

As the years passed, Lupita never wavered. When my father became ill, she was there every single step of the way. Day after day, moment after moment, she stood by him with compassion and loyalty — especially when he began to lose his independence.

My father had always been strong and capable, doing everything for himself for 81 years. Accepting help was difficult for him. But Lupita never made him feel weak — she made him feel loved.

Her kindness softened the hardest days. She understood his heart. She respected his pride. And when Dad could no longer do the things he once did, she stepped forward with quiet strength — doing what needed to be done, but always with dignity and care.

To this day, Lupita is still with us — still making our days a little easier, still keeping the gentleness of my father's spirit alive in the way she serves others. She wasn't just someone who worked for us — she became family. She still is. In the truest sense, my father lived by this silent belief:

Family isn't always given by blood — Sometimes, it is given by God.

Lupita was one of those gifts.

## A Family Foundation Rooted in God's Grace

It's easy to love when life is easy.
It is sacred to love when life is hard.

And that is what he and his siblings did.

They held each other up.
They weathered storms with grace.
They chose family, again and again.

In a world that often drifts apart, they stayed tethered —
and their connection became part of our inheritance.

A legacy of unity.
A blueprint for devotion.
A reminder that love — true love — does not fade, fracture, or forget.

"True family isn't always born — sometimes it arrives at your door, stands by your side, and loves you through every season of life."

"The heart knows what blood doesn't — who deserves a place at the table, and who deserves a place in your life."

Family is not defined only by history or last names — it's defined by presence, by loyalty, by who chooses to stay. In our home, everyone belonged. Whether through laughter on the beach, car rides through Mexico, shared meals, or quiet help during difficult times — my dad created a space where people felt safe, seen, and loved.

He didn't just raise a family...
he built a home for every soul who entered it.

To him, *family was anyone who needed love.* That was his gift — and that is his legacy.

As the years went on, we all realized something powerful:
We weren't just related — we were connected.
Not only by blood — but by heart.

Because of him,
every person who walked through his doors
knew one simple truth:

***Love makes room.***

## Legacy of Character

What we learned from my dad wasn't just how to live — it was how to treat people, how to carry ourselves with dignity, and how to face hardship without losing heart. The next chapter of his life would prove just how powerful that kind of strength truly is.

## Chapter 9

# Where Humor Met Innocence

## A Heart That Stayed Pure in a Complicated World

In life, some people shine with brilliance,
others with wisdom — and then there are those who shine with pure goodness.

My father's humor was never sharp.
It was never cut or mocked.
It was never at someone's expense.

His humor was innocent.
Soft.
Pure.

Gentle laughter meant to bring light, never shadows.

He laughed like a child discovering joy for the first time — wholehearted, genuine, and without holding anything back. His eyes sparkled when he found something funny, and sometimes just the sound of his laughter was enough to make everyone join in long before they even heard the joke.

It was impossible not to smile around him.

He didn't try to be funny — he simply was.
By nature.
By heart.

"Do You Have ESP?" — A Signature Moment

There was a phrase that became almost like a secret language between my dad and me. Whenever he would call at the exact moment I was thinking of him — or say something I secretly had on my mind — I would smile and ask:

"Dad... do you have ESP?"

Every time, with complete sincerity, he would answer:

*"Honey... do we have that cable channel? Is that part of our TV package — ESPN?"*

We would giggle every time — and even though he never quite understood what ESP meant... he lived as if he had it.

Because *somehow*, he always knew:

- When someone needed a call
- When a heart needed comfort
- When silence was wiser than words
- When laughter was the medicine the room needed

That was him.
He didn't just listen — he felt.
He didn't just hear — he understood.
His heart seemed to speak its own quiet language... one made of kindness.

One time, I told a joke with my siblings — the kind of playful humor that makes kids fall onto the floor laughing. Dad listened carefully, paused... and said with complete seriousness:

*"Honey... I don't get it."*

We laughed — not at him, but because in that moment we realized:
his innocence was sacred.
He didn't need to "get" the joke.
He was the joy.
He was the goodness we were all laughing from.

## The Diamond Ring – A Sweet Lie and a Sacred Treasure

My father never really knew how old we were. He always guessed — not because he didn't care but because age didn't matter to him. Love did.

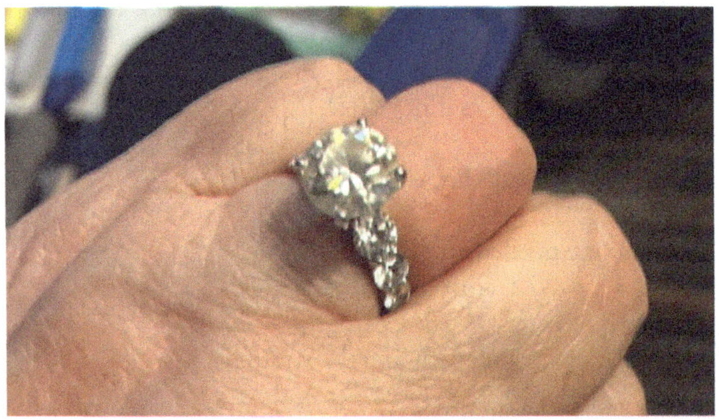

When I was 45 years old, I asked him:
"Dad... when I turn 50, would you buy me a diamond ring like Mom's?"

Without hesitation, he said:

*"Yes, honey — when you're 50, I'll get you that ring."*

A little white lie followed...
I told him that I was already turning 50.
He believed me — and took me to the store.

Years earlier, when he and my mother had celebrated their 35th wedding anniversary, he had given her a three-carat diamond ring—a treasure I had admired my whole life. At the store, he found another one just like it.

He pointed to it and said,
"This one is for your mom."

But my mother gently stopped him.
She said, *"No... that one is for Annette. I want her to have it."*

So at 45 years old, pretending to be 50, my father bought me the ring I had always dreamed of. What I didn't know then was that he would pass away when I was 47 — and he would never see my real 50th birthday.

That ring became my treasure.
Not because of the diamond...
but because of his pure-hearted love that bought it.

Toward the end of his life, I finally confessed:

*"Dad... I was never 50. I was 45 that day."*

He laughed softly... with that same pure innocence... and said:

*"I knew, honey. But I still wanted you to have it."*

## The Jeep — A Surprise He Never Saw Coming

My dad owned an old vehicle for many years. It wasn't flashy, but he loved it. It worked — and that was enough for him. But my brother and I started to feel it wasn't safe anymore.

Around that time, my-exhusband Kent bought a new Jeep — and Dad loved it instantly. So Jimmy and I decided: Dad needed a Jeep, too.

We split the cost, bought the Jeep, put a big bow on it, and brought him outside.

"Dad, this is for you," we told him.

Puzzled, he said:

> *"That Jeep belongs to Kent."*

We laughed,
"No, Dad — Kent's Jeep is gold. This one is orange. This one's yours!"

Still confused, still humble, still pure of heart, he replied:
*"Okay... but only if I get to pay you both back."*

That was him.
He couldn't accept gifts easily —
but he gave them freely every day.
Not with money.
But with kindness... time... and a heart that never stopped giving.

## His Humor Was Never Meant to Impress — Only to Love

He didn't tell jokes to be funny.
He didn't laugh to look joyful.
He was joy.
He was kindness.

He showed us what childlike purity could look like in an adult world —
what innocence looked like when it chose to survive...
and how goodness becomes strength when you let it grow
instead of hiding it.

His humor taught us that love doesn't always need to be loud.

Sometimes it just needs to be honest.

As the years unfolded, his gentle spirit continued shaping every life around him — not through grand speeches, but through quiet consistency... through everyday love.

Soon, his next greatest role would begin.
One more beautiful than any job, any title, or any adventure.

He became a grandfather.
and his love found new hands to hold.

> "The purest hearts don't always understand the world but they teach the world how to love simply by being themselves."

## Reflection -When Love Continues Beyond Goodbye

Grief is not a sign of weakness — it is a sign that love was real.

Sometimes, the hardest moments in life are not the ones we live through... but the ones we must live without are the people we love most.

If you have ever lost someone who felt like home —this chapter is for you. A Gentle Reminder :

*Grief is love with nowhere to go.*
*But with time, that love finds new paths —*
*through memories, kindness, and the way we treat others.*

Close your eyes.
Remember their voice.
Feel their embrace.
Let the tears come, if they need to...
then breathe — knowing their love never left you.

Because when love is real, it does not end.
It transforms.

## For Every Reader Who Has Loved & Lost a Loved One

This page is for you...
For the person still healing.
For the heart that still hurts.
For the memory that still lives.

May you find comfort in knowing:

- Your tears have meaning.
- Your memories matter.
- Your love is your proof — that their life still speaks.

When you laugh — they live there.
When you cherish others — they live there.
When you choose kindness — *they live there.*

Their story did not end.
It continues through you.

# Part III

# His Greatest Roles

# Chapter 10

# Papu and Lullah Bella

# A Love That Heaven Couldn't Break

✦✦✦ ═══════ ✧ ═══════ ✦✦✦

## A Bond That Saved Them Both

Some relationships do not begin with introductions...
They begin with *recognition*.
With a feeling that says, *"I already know you. I've been waiting for you."*

That was the bond between Papu and his Lulah Bella.

Lori didn't just enter the world — she entered her grandfather's heart.
She didn't just become part of the family — she became the reason he smiled again.

To others, she was a baby.
To him...
She had a renewed purpose.
She was healing in a pink blanket.
She was God saying, "There is still beauty left in this world."

She was never just his granddaughter.
She was his *Lullah Bella* –
He was her *Papu* –
Names that were more than affectionate...
They were sacred.

## The Day He Knocked – A Moment That Changed Everything

When Lori was only days old, there was a quiet morning that became a turning point in their lives.

A gentle knock on the door.
It was a man with a big heart. Papu stood there — not demanding, not imposing — but with tenderness in his eyes and love in his heart.

He simply said:
"Give me the baby. You go rest. I'll take care of her."

He took her in his arms with reverence, as if she were made of light itself. Lori was so tiny and precious — but in his arms, she felt protected, seen, and deeply adored.

From that moment on, a sacred rhythm began:
a bond of comfort, caregiving, and pure devotion.
He didn't help because he *had to* — he helped because his heart wouldn't allow her mother to walk this journey alone.

*Love, to him, was never spoken loudly.*
It was quiet.
It was daily.
It was action.

## After School – The Daily Ritual of Love

As Lori grew, so did their rituals — the kind that make a childhood magical.

Every afternoon, Papu would wait for her at Mary Help of Christians School. It didn't matter how he felt — he was always there.

"Are you hungry, Sweetheart?"
"What do you want to do today?"
"You want a snack? A little adventure?"

He didn't rush her.
He didn't hurry the moment.
He gave her time — the rarest gift of all.

Sometimes they went for a treat.
Sometimes a drive around town.
Other times just a walk in the store...
But always — laughter followed them.

Other children noticed.
They whispered,
"I wish I had a grandfather like that."

But they didn't say it with jealousy —
they said it with *awe.*

Because kindness like his is rare.
Grandfathers like him are once in a lifetime.

## Carnivals, Wonders & Childhood Magic

Whenever a carnival came to town, Papu didn't wait for permission.
He grabbed the car keys and joyfully said:
"Come on, Lullah Bella — let's go have fun."

Spinning rides.
Flashing lights.
Sticky cotton candy.
Laughter so loud it still echoes today.

He gave her a childhood *wonder.*
He taught her to never outgrow imagination.
He taught her to believe — always — in joy.

Even when the world was heavy...
He showed her that happiness could still be found.

He didn't just love her —
He *restored her spirit.*
He didn't just spoil her —
He *reminded her that the world could still be beautiful.*

## The Sweet 16 That Will Never Be Forgotten

When Lori turned sixteen, Papu celebrated her with everything his heart had.

He hosted a Sweet 16 party — a night filled with dancing, food, family, and celebration.

Lori wore a pink dress, surrounded by cousins and friends.
She felt cherished.
Seen.
Loved.

Then — a surprise that still lives in her heart today:

Papu gave her a car. Not just any car —
A Volkswagen Eos convertible. White. Beautiful. Just for her. She loved that car deeply — but even more... she loved the man who gave it.

That gift wasn't about luxury. It was his way of telling her: "I believe in you. You matter. You deserve joy." That night — she felt it with every heartbeat.

## A Love That Healed the Past

What many didn't realize was this —
Lori didn't just receive love...
She gave it back.

When Papu felt sad, when he missed someone he loved, when life felt quiet — Lori reminded him that love still existed.

She filled his lonely days with laughter.
She helped carry the weight of his grief after Jimmy passed.
She helped restore his faith in life itself.

She didn't know it at the time —
but she saved him
just as much as he saved her.

Their bond was not ordinary —
It was a divine appointment,
written by God before she was ever born.

## A Love That Leaves a Legacy

Even now —
when Lori speaks of Papu,
her voice softens.

She smiles.
She sometimes cries.
But she carries him in every step she takes.

Because he didn't just love with words — he loved with his life.

That kind of love...never dies.

It becomes a legacy.
It becomes strength.
It becomes the reason we keep going.

> "
> Some people touch your life for a moment. Others leave fingerprints on your soul forever.

# Chapter 11
# The Family HeBuilt

## A Legacy of Gathered Hearts

Family was never an obligation for Ernesto Ramirez — it was his calling. He didn't just belong to a family — he built one.

Raised in a house with ten children, he learned early on that love didn't need luxury to grow — it only needed presence, loyalty, and a place at the table. As he grew older, he carried that belief everywhere he went.

He gathered people the way a shepherd gathers sheep — never leaving anyone behind.

To Papu, *family wasn't just "who you were born to"*.

It was who you made room for in your heart.
Cousins, in-laws, neighbors, housekeepers, friends — all became part of his circle. And once you were in, you stayed in. That was his gift.

## Easter — The Holy Gathering

There was one time of year when his love for family shined the brightest: Easter.

Easter was not just a holiday —
It was a reunion of hearts.

It was the day everyone knew:
*We're going to the ranch.*
*We're going to be together.*
*We're going to laugh, eat, tell stories... and remember who we are.*

Most years, it was held at Aunt Gloria's or Aunt Julieta's ranch, where nearly 75 family members gathered — siblings, spouses, children, grandchildren, neighbors, and friends... all stitched together by love and laughter. The Ramirez history stood side by side — the past, present, and future sharing one picnic table.

The smell of barbecue filled the air.
Kids ran in every direction.
Adults pulled folding chairs into circles of conversation.
Stories were told.
Food was shared.
Hearts were full.

When the softball game began — the real holiday started.
Easter softball games were legendary. Every year, it started with friendly smiles... and often ended with playful arguments. A little competitive spirit — some shouting, some laughter, maybe one or two stomped feet — but always... always forgiveness before the sun went down.

Because in this family — love won by nightfall.

The kids rode four-wheelers across the ranch, chasing the last light of evening. Easter egg hunts scattered across the fields as laughter echoed through the trees. Without fail — one person always transformed the day into magic...

Cousin Ricky — the Easter Bunny.

He loved surprising the children, dressed and ready to delight every little heart. When the kids saw him hopping around in that costume, they didn't just see an Easter Bunny...they saw joy.

They saw childhood.
They saw another reason to love their family.

For Papu, these were holy moments. Not because of tradition... but because the whole family was together, just like when they were young.

It wasn't just a holiday — it was home.

## Christmas – The Quiet Love

While Easter was loud and full of laughter —
Christmas was quiet, warm, and sacred.

At Christmas, the noise faded, and tenderness took its place.

After my grandmother — *my mother's mother* — came to live with us, it became tradition that she would cook Christmas dinner, no matter how tired she was. She loved being in the kitchen — flour on her apron, music humming in the background, pots simmering on the stove.

Mom would help...
Lupita would join... I would be there beside them — another set of hands in the rhythm of family.

Dad was often working during Christmas.
But no matter how busy his day was...
He made time to come home for dinner — even if just for an hour.

He didn't rush the meal.
He didn't complain about work.
He simply sat at the table, smiled, and said the same beautiful words every holiday:

After dinner, even if he had to go back to work — he left us full — of food, yes — but more importantly...full of love.

## When Families Change

As time passed and life shifted, so did the family gatherings.
The Easter celebrations became smaller. Some siblings grew ill. Some passed on. Some cousins moved away, and busy schedules replaced open weekends.

Slowly, our gatherings became memories rather than plans.

There came a moment when I said:
"*We need one more reunion.*
*We need to try.*"

So I organized a family gathering... invited 50 cousins... only about 25 came.

Not out of lack of love — but because life changes.

People grow apart.
Schedules fill.
Years move faster than we expect them to.

Yet — even with only half the number... that reunion mattered.
Laughter still echoed.
Memories were shared.
Stories were told through tears and smiles.

It reminded us all that roots do not vanish.

They may stretch farther apart —
but they remain connected beneath the ground.

Somewhere in those stories...we still felt him.
We still knew what home felt like.
Because he built it.

## His Real Legacy

It wasn't money.
It wasn't land.
It wasn't possessions.

It was people.
It was love shared and passed on.
It was moments that made us feel like we belonged.

His legacy was found in:

- children remembering the Easter hunts,
- adults remembering his humor,
- cousins remembering his hugs,
- neighbors remembering his generosity,
- Lupita remembering his compassion,
- and all of us remembering his voice saying:

"Come in — my house is your house." He didn't build an empire.
He built something greater...a family that loved because they were loved.

That is the rarest treasure of all.

## Reflection – The Family That Love Built

He taught us:

- That gatherings matter.
- That meals taste better when shared.
- That family doesn't need perfection — only presence.
- That laughter after an argument is the sound of healing.
- That the strongest memories don't need cameras — only hearts.

He showed us that home is not a building—it is the sound of your name spoken with love.

When we think about him now...
We don't remember what he wore.
We don't count what he owned.
We don't recite his titles.

We remember his voice.
We remember his hands.
We remember how every person in the room felt seen when he walked in.

Because when a man loves like that...
his legacy is not written in stone...

It is written in people.

> "
> The greatest houses are not built with bricks – but with hearts that know how to make room for each other.
>
> In loving memory of
> Ernesto Ramirez

# Chapter 12
# A Heart Bigger Than Texas

## His Generosity, His Legacy, His Way of Loving Others

Where do I begin? This is the story I have carried in my heart for the last five years — the story I spoke about with Father Anthony the day I told him, *"I want to write about my dad."* He looked at me and said, "Then sit down and do it. God will tell you when the time is right."

Back then, I didn't know how. I didn't know if I was ready.
But life has a way of preparing the heart for healing, even when healing feels far away.

After walking through my own storms — moments when hope felt blurry and God felt distant — I realized the time had come. Not just to tell his story... but to understand it. To see it not just through memory — but through meaning.

Because my father, Ernesto Ramirez, was more than a good man.

He was a giver. A provider. A gentle protector of human dignity.
And the first thing I would tell you is this:

He had a heart bigger than Texas.

## Love Didn't Wait for Money to Arrive

When we were young, life was humble. My dad worked hard, but money didn't always stretch far. Our Christmas trees didn't have many presents beneath them. Maybe one or two gifts. But they were special, because they were his best — and we knew it.

There was beauty in that simplicity.
I knew what it felt like to not have much...but I also knew what it felt like to have everything that truly mattered — love, safety, and family.

On Christmas mornings, I would run next door to the Valls family — a home full of toys, four children, and excitement. I loved playing with their gifts... but I never felt jealousy. I felt joy. Because I had something money couldn't buy — a father who loved me well.

Later in life, things changed.
The Bruni Mineral Trust — the family's oil and gas inheritance — began to produce steady income. That's when life shifted. Travel became possible. Opportunities opened. And slowly... carefully... my father began to build his vision.

But he never forgot those simple Christmases.
He never forgot what it meant to have little — and still give much.
That memory shaped how he treated people for the rest of his life.

## Building a Legacy, One Brick of Love at a Time

As money began to come in, he moved with intention — patiently, wisely. He began to invest in real estate — one house at a time. He'd buy it, fix it, pay it off... then move on to the next one.

This wasn't ambition. It was protection.
He wanted his family to have security.
He wanted his children to stand strong.
So he built — slowly, steadily, faithfully.

About 30 years ago, he looked at me and said:
**"You need something of your own. You need roots. Let's build something."**

That's how it began. He built a **10-unit apartment complex**, which became known as *Lori's Apartments.* Later, we built *Papu Land* — a partnership created in honor of my father, whose nickname was Papu.

That wasn't business.
That was a legacy.
That was a father's way of saying, *"I want you to stand tall long after I am gone."*

## A Generous Heart — Quiet, Steady, Unconditional

The more he built, the more he gave. Money never owned him — it fueled his kindness.

✔ When his barber was struggling financially — Dad helped.
✔ When Mary Help of Christians School needed funds — Dad gave.
✔ When friends and family couldn't pay for trips to Mexico — Dad paid for everyone.
✔ When my mother-in-law moved to Laredo — he kept her car full of gas.

He never needed recognition.
His generosity was *quiet... humble... discreet.*
He lived by a simple rule: "If you have more than enough, then someone around you probably needs help."

Even children at Lori's school saw it. They'd tell their friends,
*"I wish I had a grandfather like Papu."*

Because kindness doesn't need words.
It just needs presence.

## Lessons From the Apartment Complex

When Dad began renting out apartments, he made rules — respectful ones. Everyone deserved dignity. Everyone deserved a chance. But when times were hard... when someone lost their job, or suffered an illness, or lost a family member... Dad would look at them and say gently:

"Don't worry. Pay when you can. God will provide."

He always did.

There were times when I took over and noticed people struggling. My heart remembered the simple Christmases. I remembered how Dad provided when we had little. I would wait. I would be patient.
Because compassion is an inheritance, too.

Some inherit money.
Others inherit wisdom.
But Dad left us something far greater: a way of treating people.

## The Quiet Empire He Built

What looked like wise investments...
Were really acts of protection.
What looked like business decisions...
Were really acts of love.

But if you asked him how he built his "empire", he'd simply smile and say: "With God, everything is possible."

Because faith was his foundation.
Generosity was his language.

He never chased wealth. He simply believed...that when God gives you more — it's because He trusts you to share it well.

## What He Truly Left Behind

In the end, I realized something:
Dad didn't just build a financial legacy.
He built something far greater.

- He built a legacy of kindness.
- He built generational humility.
- He built a standard for love that lives on in us.

When he passed, people didn't thank him for his success. They thanked him for his heart. They remembered his smile. They felt his gentleness. They called him what he truly was:

An angel on earth.

And now, I see the truth so clearly. His generosity wasn't about money. His legacy wasn't about land.

His legacy was love.
Love — the kind he gave — never dies.

## Reflection – What My Father Taught Me

I once believed legacy was measured by what we leave behind—
but now I understand: Legacy is what we leave *within* others.

My father didn't just teach me how to invest.
He taught me how to believe.
He didn't just provide shelter.
He taught me how to create a home.

One of the greatest lessons he passed on came through his real estate work — not through contracts or paperwork— but through *people.*

When tenants fell behind on rent, most landlords would have sent warnings or demands.

But not my dad.
He didn't begin with judgment.
He began with understanding.

He would say:

> *"Times get hard, honey.*
> *Sometimes people just need a little time.*
> *If they're honest with you—*
> *be patient with them.*
> *God always provides."*

He showed me that business decisions must not only be logical—
they must be humane.

So when someone lost a job, became ill, or fell behind for a reason beyond their control, he would wait.

He believed that respect builds bridges. Dignity—when given—often comes back multiplied.

Today, I carry that lesson forward.
When someone is honest with me and says,
"*I need a little time,*"
I remember my dad, and I answer with compassion.

Because I now understand:
Numbers don't build communities.
People do.

Most tenants eventually manage to pay—
not because they were pressured,
but because they were treated with dignity.

My father helped me see that true leadership
doesn't just manage problems...it honors people.

So, I walk forward with this truth he instilled in me:
You don't just run a business with your mind.
You run it with your heart.

"True wealth isn't what you keep – it's what you give away in love.

He didn't just tell me to love people—
He showed me how.
Through patience.
Through quiet courage.
Through unconditional giving.

When people speak his name today, they don't talk about his success—
they talk about how he made them feel:

Safe. Seen. Respected. Loved.

Now I know...that is the truest form of inheritance.

# CHAPTER 13
# The Gentleman in the Details

## *The Quiet Ways He Built a World of Love*

Some men leave their mark through achievements.
Others leave it through words or reputation.
But my father — Ernesto Ramírez — left his mark through the details.

The little things.

The small habits.
The quiet routines.
The gestures are so simple that you might miss them if you weren't paying attention.

Yet... those were the very things that revealed the gentleman he truly was.

From the outside, he appeared soft-spoken, humble, reserved. But inside, he carried a world of love, responsibility, intention, and grace. The details of his life — his devotion to family, his craftsmanship, his traditions, his rituals — painted the truest portrait of the man behind the legacy.

Those details, when woven together, tell a story that is every bit as important as the grand chapters of travel, leadership, or fatherhood.

They were proof that goodness doesn't need applause.
It just needs consistency.

## Saturday Evenings: Faith, Habit, and a Rocking Pew

Every Saturday evening, without fail, you could find him at the 6:30 p.m. Mass at *San Martín de Porras Church.* It was his anchor — the place where he gathered himself, his thoughts, and his gratitude before another week began.

We would sit together in the pew, quiet and reverent... until suddenly, we felt it.

Rocking.
Gentle at first... then more.
Then a steady back-and-forth rhythm.

We would whisper, trying not to laugh:
"Dad... stop rocking the pew!"

His feet would tap, his body would sway, and without knowing it, he'd be rocking the entire wooden bench — and everyone sitting on it. It was innocent. It was funny.

It was so him.
A small detail... yet one of the memories that makes us smile the most.
Mass was never rushed. Never an obligation. It was a ritual — a quiet promise between him and God. When Mass was over, another tradition followed.

## Luby's and Simple Joys

If Sundays were restful, Saturdays were predictable in the best way: Church, then dinner at Luby's.

It wasn't fancy. He didn't care.
He loved the simplicity — the trays, the conversations, the routine, the certainty that his family was together.

Some people measure luxury by price.
My father measured it by presence.

Those dinners, simple as they were, became priceless memories.

## His Hands Built More Than a Home

Before my parents were even married, he had already begun building the house that would become our family home. When they finally married and moved in, he never stopped adding to it — improving it, shaping it, molding it.

Brick by brick, board by board.
With his own two hands.

Later came the master bedroom — a space he designed and built himself.

Then the backyard shed.
Then the covered patio.

He didn't need contractors.
He was a contractor, carpenter, designer, and builder.
Every corner of that home had his fingerprints on it.
Every room held a story.
Every nail, every beam, every stroke of paint was an act of love.

This was not just a house.

It was a testament to commitment — and the quiet pride of a man who believed that providing for his family was the greatest honor a father could have.

## Movie Nights: A Neighborhood of Kids, a Projector, and Popcorn

One of the most magical details of his life came from something so simple... movies.

On weekends, especially during our childhood, he would bring home a commercial-grade projector — the kind used by the television station where he worked. Later, he even had one of his own.

Then came the reels. Big, round, old-school film reels.
Kid-friendly movies. Classics. Films that made the whole neighborhood run to our house.

He turned our home into a movie theater.
Popcorn, blankets, pillows, excited whispers — all the neighborhood kids piled in for the show.

But the real comedy came from Jimmy.

He and Dad were mischievous partners in crime. Whenever a scary part in the movie was about to happen, Jimmy would run to Dad and whisper: "Turn off the lights now!"

Dad would flick the switch —
Total darkness.
Screams.

Pillows flying.
Kids jumping onto each other.

Chaos, laughter, memories we still talk about to this day.

Through it all, Dad would sit in the back... smiling... watching us more than he watched the movie.

Because *our joy* was his favorite show.

## Summer Days: Bubbles, Backyard Pools & Neighborhood Laughter

Summers brought new "projects," as he called them.

He assembled backyard pools — big, inflatable ones — and filled them to the brim so we could splash around. Sometimes, someone would pour in Mr. Bubbles... and suddenly the pool was a giant bath full of foam and squealing kids.

The neighborhood children flocked to our yard.
Dad let them in without hesitation.

There was enough joy to go around.

Somehow, even after long days at work, he'd find time to stand outside and watch the chaos — making sure everyone was safe, everyone was happy, everyone belonged.

## The State Fair of Texas — His Unskippable Tradition

Every year when the State Fair of Texas opened in Dallas, Dad was ready. He'd take me and Jimmy when we were young, exploring every booth, every ride, every new attraction. But even when we were older and didn't always want to go, he still went — by himself if he had to.

Why?
Because he loved seeing what was new:

The cars.
The trucks.
The latest models.

He could walk around the auto exhibits for hours, studying every detail, every design, every innovation.

It wasn't about buying anything.
It was about wonder — about staying curious, young at heart.

## The Gentleman Revealed Through a Thousand Little Things

People often think "gentleman" means polished or wealthy or sophisticated.
But Dad taught us a different definition:

A gentleman is someone who listens.
Who pays attention.
Who shows up.
Who builds with his hands.
Who prays with his heart.
Who helps without being asked.
Who sees children as blessings.
Who treats workers, neighbors, tenants, strangers — as equals.
Who never complains, even when tired.

A gentleman is a man whose goodness can be seen in his smallest actions.
Those small things — the pew rocking, the movie nights, the home projects, the State Fair trips — they were threads woven into the fabric of his character.

They were reminders that love is rarely loud.
More often... it is steady.

Quiet.
Faithful.
Unseen by the world, but unforgettable to the people who live inside it.

## A Life Shaped by Grace, Work, and Quiet Strength

He lived with a heart big enough to hold everyone he loved —
and this chapter reveals the quiet details that made that heart unforgettable.
Together, these memories lead us gently into what comes next:
the farewell...
the letting go...
the grief...
and the legacy of love he left behind.

He lived well.
He loved well.
He left us more than memories.
He left us a blueprint for a beautiful life.

# Part IV
# The Farewell and the Legacy

# Chapter 14
# The Last Goodbye

✦✦✦ ═══════ ✧ ═══════ ✦✦✦

## Where Heaven Met Earth One Final Time

Where do I begin?

This is the chapter I never wanted to write — yet always knew I would. The chapter that requires courage, memory, and faith. The one where a daughter must do the hardest thing in the world... love her father enough to let him go.

For months, I knew this moment would come — but no amount of knowing prepares you for the truth of it. When life begins to whisper that time is running short, the heart begs to hold on. But sometimes, love takes a different shape.

Sometimes, the bravest act of love... is release.

Because I believe with all my heart... This goodbye was not an ending.
It was a homecoming.

## Whispers of Heaven

Before his illness, life felt steady. My father — strong, giving, full of heart — was our pillar. But slowly, we began to notice his strength fading. He grew weaker. Walking became harder. Concern turned into hospital visits... and hospital visits turned into tests.

One doctor looked at me and said quietly,
*"I hope it isn't what we think it is."*

But it was.
Lymphoma.
A word that changed everything in a single breath.
While he stayed in the hospital, I found a book lying nearby — 90 Minutes in Heaven.

I began to read it, and somehow... I knew.
I felt God was preparing me.
Softening my heart for what I didn't want to face.

We didn't talk about dying. Not yet.
But something inside us both began to shift.
Love became softer.
Time felt sacred.
Silence became prayer.

## His Heart Was Ready Before We Were

One night, sitting beside him, he took my hand and said quietly,
"Annette... it's time for me to go home."

I froze. I begged him softly,
"Dad... not today. Please. Not today."

But over time, I realized something profound:
He wasn't giving up.
He was accepting grace.

He had fought illness with courage — but now, he was ready for peace.

A few months later, when his health declined again, we knew it was time. He was hospitalized once more — and our whole family gathered.

Around 2 a.m., I sent everyone home to rest. It was just us. Just his baby girl and her father — the way so much of life had been.

He looked at me and said it again — not with fear, but with clarity:
"Annette... I need to go home."

This time, God gave me the strength to answer:
"Yes, Dad. You are going home — to heaven — to rejoice with your Father God... with Jimmy... with your family. You are going to a beautiful place."

He smiled.
He rested.
Peace came.

## A Visit From Heaven – Aunt Gloria

The final hours were sacred. What happened next... feels like something the world might doubt — but faith understands.

As he lay in the hospital bed, too weak to stand or speak for long... his eyes began to move toward the ceiling. A softness came over him. A glow, almost. Then he said something that sent chills down my spine:

"Gloria... you came for me."

Aunt Gloria — his beloved sister who had passed just six months earlier.

He spoke to her as if she were standing right beside him. For hours, he talked — to someone only he could see. It was one of the most beautiful things I've ever witnessed.

Not frightening. Not strange. Just... holy.
At one point, he said he needed to repay her a debt he owed. It made us laugh softly through tears... even in that sacred moment, his integrity remained. That was my dad — even at heaven's door, he wanted to make things right.

I believe with all my heart that he was not alone in that room.
Heaven was close.

## The Last Breath

The next morning, Dr. Godínez came to the hospital. My cousin Chacha was there, too. The room was quiet, calm — but not heavy. Something soft had settled in the air. Something holy... peaceful... almost glowing.

The doctor looked at us and said gently,
"Watch how he's breathing... peacefully. He's ready."

We watched.
He breathed.
And then...
he didn't.

Just like that — without pain, without struggle — my father took his last breath.

But it did not feel like an ending.
It felt like a door opening.
Like heaven had reached down — and taken his hand.

## The Hardest Thing I've Ever Done

After he passed, I knew it was time to tell my mother. I walked out of the room holding the weight of the world... and the peace of heaven...
all at once.

Yet — there were no regrets.
It was Dad... and his baby girl... at the end.
Just as it had been in the beginning.

Family and friends came soon after. They said goodbye not to a man — but to a *legacy of love.* Stories poured in. Tears fell. Arms held one another. The room was full of grief... but bigger still — gratitude.

There are no words worthy enough...
to thank everyone who came.
To thank God for allowing such a goodbye.
To thank life... for giving us him.

## What I Know Now

I used to think death was an ending.
But now I know — it is a homecoming.

My father did not disappear.
He did not fade.
He simply changed addresses — from earth...
to heaven.

I believe, with everything in me — that one day, he will meet me again. Not in a hospital room... but in a place where laughter never ends and tears no longer belong.

> "
> The ones we love never truly leave us – they simply move into our hearts, where love becomes eternal.

Until then...
I carry his love forward.
I live the way he taught me —
with kindness, with generosity, with faith.

Because the greatest way to honor someone you love...
is to live the lessons they left behind.

# Chapter 15
# Heaven's Angel Continuing His Love From Above

## Faith, Presence, and the Promise of Forever Love

There are chapters in life that close quietly...
and others that leave us breathless.

Losing my father was the kind that takes the air out of your lungs.
It felt as if time paused—as if the world kept moving but I stood still.
For the first time in my life...
the gentle giant was gone.

He wasn't just a father —
he was the calm when everything felt chaotic,
the laughter when life felt heavy,
and the steady presence that always made us feel safe.

# When He Left, So Did Our Easy Joy

Grief has a way of filling every room —
even the silent ones.
You can be surrounded by people and still feel alone,
because the one voice you need is the one that has gone quiet.

After my dad passed away, I felt as if the world had lost its color.
Even the simplest tasks felt heavy — waking up, walking into his house,
seeing an empty house that is without him.

He used to visit me and Lori often —
and we had a tradition.
We would all lie in bed together — he, Lori, and I —
sometimes watching TV...
sometimes just talking...
sometimes simply enjoying each other's presence with the dogs nearby.

Those weren't just moments.
They were home.
They were comfortable.
They were love — the kind you don't fully understand until it's gone.

Then one day, it ended.
The bed felt too big.
The air felt too quiet.
Life felt like a puzzle with a missing piece — a piece we could never replace.

I cried until I had no more tears.
I cried because the world felt different.
I cried because I didn't know how to live without him.
I cried because I couldn't imagine a day where his voice
wouldn't echo in my heart.

## When Lori Spoke for Him

One day, in the middle of my tears, Lori said to me gently:

"Mom... you have to stop crying. Papu keeps coming to me.
He tells me, 'Tell your mom I'm okay. Tell her I'm in a good place.
Tell her to stop crying — I can't see her cry anymore.'"

I froze.
It felt as if the world stood still again—
but this time, in a different way.

Because maybe...
just maybe...
he wasn't far away at all.

Maybe heaven was closer than I thought.
Maybe God was still giving us ways to hear his voice.
Maybe... love doesn't end when life does.

## The Place Where Grief Met Grace

In those first weeks after my dad passed away, I didn't know where to go with my pain. The world felt too loud, my heart felt too heavy, and home felt too empty. So I went somewhere quiet — somewhere sacred.

For 30 days straight, I found myself at the Adoration Chapel at St. Patrick's Church. That small room became my refuge. I would walk in, sit before the Blessed Sacrament, and every day I would cry, and every day, I would tell myself:

"Go in. Cry. Let it out.
When you walk out — be a little stronger than yesterday."

There was something healing about that space. In the silence, I felt his presence. In the stillness, I felt God's mercy. Some days I didn't have words — only tears — but I knew God could understand the language of my heart.

One day, while sitting there quietly, a woman gently approached me. She didn't know my story, but she could see the pain in my eyes. She placed her hand softly on mine and handed me a flower.

I broke down again.
But this time... it wasn't from pain alone.
It was from comfort.
It was from peace.
It was from knowing — God had heard me... and maybe my dad had too.

That chapel became the bridge between my broken heart and my healing.
It didn't erase the grief... but it reminded me that I was never alone in it.

## Living With His Absence and His Presence

There is a moment in grief when you realize love never truly leaves.
It simply steps into a new dimension.

Yes, there were days we felt a hole in our hearts —
a place that nothing and no one could fill.
But as time passed, that hole became something different.
It became a doorway.

A sacred place where memories continued living.
A space where we could still talk to him...
still feel him...
still love him.

In that quiet space, we learned a powerful truth:

Death ends a life — but it does not end a relationship.
The bond remains.
The love continues.
The lessons still speak.

Only the form changes.

## Faith That Was Never Loud — But Always Strong

My dad believed in God with the kind of faith that didn't need to be spoken.
It lived in the way he treated others.
It showed in his patience.
It echoed in every gentle action.

Now, with him gone,
we also trust —
that he is in God's hands still.

## Heaven Did Not Take Him Away — It Completed Him

Maybe heaven isn't far.
Maybe it's as close as our next act of kindness.
As close as the next laugh shared.
As close as the next prayer whispered.

Heaven did not erase his light — it amplified it.

Now his love flows through us in a thousand gentle ways:

When someone forgives quickly.
When someone helps a stranger.
When someone smiles through tears.
When someone chooses faith over fear."

That's him.
Still teaching.
Still loving.
Still shining.

## A Love That Lives Forever

Even though life will never be the same, we find comfort in this truth:

He may not walk beside us anymore— but he walks within us now.

We carry him in every generous act.
In every gentle word.
In every shared smile.
In every moment we choose kindness over judgment.

His legacy wasn't just love.
It was a way of life.
A way of being.
A way of seeing the world — with grace and gratitude.

We miss him deeply.
We feel his absence every day.
But his spirit fills every empty space.

Because when love is real...
it never truly leaves.

It simply finds a new way to stay.

## A Daughter's Heart — Writing Through the Hurt

Today, as I write these words, my heart still aches for my father.
The missing never goes away — it simply becomes quieter, woven into the rhythm of everyday life. There are days when the memory of his voice brings comfort... and days when it brings tears. But even with the heaviness, I knew I had to write this book.

I am writing through the grief, through the love, through the ache — because I want my father's legacy to live beyond me, beyond Lori, beyond our family.

I want his story to be preserved for generations, marked on the world in the same beautiful way he marked every life he touched.

I write this also for every person who picks up this book with their own loss tucked inside their heart. I want them to know:

When someone leaves this world with love,
their presence doesn't disappear —
it transforms.

It lives in the memories they gifted us,
in the lessons they whispered,
in the way they shaped our hearts
and softened our souls.

Their story becomes part of our story.

So even when the tears come,
I hold on to that truth —
and I hope you will too.

Because love this pure... never ends.
It simply continues in a different way,
carried gently in the people who remain.

> "
> **Those we love**
> **don't go away–**
> **they walk beside us**
> **every day.**
> **Unseen, unheard,**
> **but always near–**
> **still loved, still missed,**
> **and forever dear.**

# Chapter 16
# Letters to Heaven

## A Collection of Love, Memory & Eternal Connection

For the man whose life touched countless hearts, and whose spirit continues to guide us from above.

These letters are written with gratitude, with longing, with laughter, and with the kind of love that does not end when a life ends... only when the remembering stops —and we will never stop remembering you.

## Memories from Dr. Patrick Valls

*Next-Door Neighbor & Family Friend*

I grew up next door to Annette on Stewart Street, and in many ways, I have always considered her a sister. Our families were connected long before we were born — Ernesto and my father, Alfonso, each one of ten children, first lived as neighbors and friends on San Bernardo Street in downtown Laredo.

Later, both families moved to Stewart Street, where their friendship — and ours — continued for generations.

From my earliest memories, I knew Ernesto as a gentle, mild-mannered, and kind man. Unlike most adults in our neighborhood, he would ask us to call him by his first name — "Just call me Ernie," he would say with a smile. Even as a child, I felt seen, heard, and respected around him. He didn't speak to us — he spoke with us.
And that small difference made us feel important.

What impressed me most was his work ethic and humility. I watched him come home after a full day at the television station — and instead of resting, he would roll up his sleeves and keep working. He built a laundry room and garage storage area with his own hands... and later, he went on to construct an entire master bedroom — doing all the carpentry himself. No contractors. No helpers. Just quiet skill, determination, and pride in his work.

He had an artist's touch — never flashy, always practical — and while he kept things simple for himself, he always provided the very best for his family.

Some of my favorite memories of Ernie were the movie nights he hosted for all the neighborhood kids. He would borrow a commercial-grade projector from the TV station and bring home reels of films — many that had been, or would soon be, aired on television.

We felt like VIP guests every time. There was popcorn, excitement, laughter — and the happiest kind of silence when the
lights went off and the movie began.

But what I remember most was the way he looked at us during the movies — with a soft smile, a quiet joy, as though nothing made him happier than watching children feel wonder.

That's who Ernie was:
A man who worked hard...
Who built things with his hands...

Who spoke with kindness...
Who treated children with respect...
Who spread joy not with words...
...but with presence.

For me, he was more than a neighbor.
He was an example.
A role model.
A kind heart I'll never forget.

---

## Memories from From Ricky & Sylvia Benavides Remembered Through the Eyes of Those Who Loved Him

*Dear Ernie,*

*We've been thinking about you — the way you laughed, the way you spoke, the way you carried yourself with kindness that didn't need words. Annette asked us to share a few memories, but the truth is... once we start talking about you, the memories come like waves. You left that kind of mark.*

*We remember the stories you used to tell about going to the baseball games — both here "down the rail" and across in Mexico. You always had a way of describing those games so vividly that we felt like we were sitting right there with you, hearing the cheers, smelling the popcorn, watching the dust rise from the field. Baseball wasn't just a sport to you — it was joy, companionship, and a piece of your youth you loved to revisit.*

*Then there were your stories of the Texas State Fair in Dallas. You talked about them with such excitement — the rides, the food, the new cars on display. You would describe every detail as if you were still the young man walking through the fairgrounds with wide eyes and a full heart. We could always tell how much those memories meant to you.*

*What we remember most, though, is your gentle soul. You were a loving father, a devoted husband, and a man whose kindness was felt before it was spoken. There's one moment we will never forget.*

*When Mrs. Benavides was dying, you walked into the room, leaned close to her, and said in that soft, loving voice: "¿Qué tienes, chiquita?*

*I need you to get better... What are we going to do without you?"*

*Your words weren't dramatic.*

*They were tender.*
*They were real.*
*They were you.*

*Another memory we treasure is from beach vacations. Everyone would rush to put on their swimsuits, eager to run to the ocean... except you. You moved at your own peaceful pace. Then — on the last day of the trip, while everyone else was checking out — suddenly you were ready to go to the swimming pool. It made us laugh then, and it makes us smile now. That was your charm — you lived life the way your heart guided you.*

*Oh, the parties.*
*At every celebration Mrs. Benavides hosted, you were there — present, smiling, supportive — always wearing one of your guayabera shirts. It became part of your signature look. You didn't need to be the loudest in the room; your presence itself was comfort. You were steady. You were constant. You were loved. We could talk about you all night, Ernie.*

*There are too many stories, too many moments, too many memories that still bring warmth to our hearts. But for now, we send this letter to heaven with love, gratitude, and a smile — knowing you are watching over the family you adored.*

*Until we meet again,*
*Ricky & Sylvia Benavides*

# Letter to Heaven From Your Daughter

There are no words to express how I was the luckiest girl in the world to have you as my father. Even after all these years, it still feels like you just left us yesterday. Not a day passes that I don't think of you... wish for your presence... or pray for your guidance.

There are so many moments in my life — decisions about business, family, and everyday challenges — when I close my eyes and imagine what you would say. I still long to hear your voice, your steady wisdom, the calm way you always made everything feel possible. But one thing I hold onto, Dad — with pride, with gratitude, with love — is that
I learned from the best.
I learned by watching you:
your patience,
your kindness,
your work ethic,
your loyalty,
your unwavering love for family.

Every day, I try my best to live by the example you set. Thank you for teaching me what love truly looks like. Thank you for showing me what family really means. Thank you for shaping my heart with your gentleness, generosity, and goodness.

You taught me how to be strong without hardness...
how to give without expecting anything back...
how to put family first...
how to trust God even when life feels heavy...
and how to choose joy in simple moments.

Dad, I miss you deeply — more than words can ever say.
But I carry you with me in everything I do, in every decision I make,
in every act of kindness I offer.

Your legacy is alive in me.
As long as I breathe...
I will honor you.

I will keep telling your story.
I will keep living with the heart you taught me to have.
I will keep loving the way you loved —
fully, gently, and without conditions.

Until the day God calls me home and I see you again...

I love you, Dad.
Forever your daughter,
Annette.

# A Note of Thanks and a Prayer of Love

# *A Thank You to My Dad*

*Thank you, Dad, for every trip, every adventure, every moment you turned into a memory.*

*Thank you for teaching me that the world is full of beauty — not just in places, but in people. Because of you, I learned to welcome life with open arms, to trust the journey, and to believe that there is joy waiting around every corner.*

*You didn't just give us trips — you gave us a way to live.*

*You didn't just take us traveling —you took us home to ourselves.*

*I will carry your adventures for the rest of my life.*

*And wherever I go...*
*I'll look for you in the sunrise.*
*Because I know —*
*that's where you'll be.*

# Prayer for Those Who Grieve

Lord,
Comfort those who grieve and
carry broken hearts gently
in Your hands.

Thank you to fathers who walk
through loss with grace, who
keep loving when it hurts, and
who show us what true strength
looks like.

May Jimmy's memory be a blessing that
lives on in all of us, and may Papu's
resilience teach
us to hold onto faith through
every storm.

Help us honor those we've lost
by living with comppassion,
tenderness, and
love - just as he

Amen.

✦✧✦

# Memories That Will Forever Live in Our Hearts

IMPERIAL PALA
OIL COMPA

# Golden Roots

# A Record of Family and Legacy

# The Golden Roots

**PATRICK HENRY**

"Give me liberty, or give me death." – American Founder

**CONCELACIÓN HENRY**

Descendant of Henry Family Line
Strength • Honor • Legacy

**ANTONIO MATEO (A.M.) BRUNI**

Founder of the Bruni Mineral Trust • Pioneer Oil • Gas • Uranium • South Texas History

**HERLINDA BRUNI RAMÍREZ**

Daughter of Concelación Henry & A.M. Bruni • Mother of Ernesto Ramírez
Bridge Between Two Powerful Bloodlines • Heart of the Bruni Heritage

## The Heart of the Tree – Papu

**ERNESTO RAMÍREZ**

A Heart Bigger Than Texas • Protector • Provider • Humble Gentleman • Trustee of the Bruni Mineral Trust • Builder • Legacy Maker • Angel on Earth

## The Next Generation

**JIMMY RAMÍREZ**

Beloved Son • Forever Missed
A Light in Our Hearts

**ANNETTE RAMÍREZ**

Daughter • Storykeeper • Author
Preserving His Legacy

## The Legacy Continues

**ADRIAN**

Scholar • Leader

**MIGUEL "JELLYBEAN**

A Heart Big as Papu's

**LULLAH BELLA**

Named in Papu's Honor
"Lulabella"

*A Heritage Of Love And Light*

"From our roots we find strength... from our ancestors we find purpose."

# FAMILY HISTORY NOTES

*An Heirloom Appendix for the Ramirez–Bruni–Henry Legacy*

## SECTION 1 — The Bruni Mineral Trust Legacy

| Heritage Element | Details |
|---|---|
| **Founder** | **A.M. Bruni** — an early South Texas visionary Oil • Gas • Uranium |
| **Industries Impact** | exploration Later provided mineral support that helped Ernesto |
| **on Family** | invest wisely and<br>build stability<br>Not for extravagance — but for establishing a |
| **Purpose** | |
| **Connection to Ernesto** | |
| | Enabled opportunities that he turned into generosity, real<br>estate<br>investments, and security for future generations *lasting family foundation* |

## SECTION 2 — Patrick Henry Connection

## (Historical Footnote)

*A Legacy of Courage and Conviction*

| Historical Reference | Details |
|---|---|
| **Maternal Lineage** | Through **Concelación Henry**mother of Arlinda Bruni Ramirez |
| **Possible Ancestral Link** | **Patrick Henry**FoundingFather of the United States |
| **Famous Declaration** | *"Give me liberty, or give me death!"* |
| **Influence on Ernesto** | Reflected in his quiet strength, personal integrity, and unwavering responsibility |

| | |
|---|---|
| **Notes** | Whether confirmed or preserved through family oral history, it illuminates a spirit of resilience and honor |

## SECTION 3 — The Legacy He Built

*Values Carried Through a Lifetime*

| Value He Taught | How He Lived This Value |
|---|---|
| Responsibility | Worked multiple jobs • Built his own home • Provided without |
| Patience | complaint Gave tenants grace • Understood hardship • Extended |
| Compassion | kindness first Saved animals • Helped neighbors • Lifted others |
| Faith Unity | quietly Prayed before decisions • Trusted God through every season |
| | Family first • Peacemaker • Kept relationships whole and warm |

**"Legacy is not what we leave behind —**
**but what we leave *within* the hearts of others."**

## SECTION 4 — Future Generations

*Where Will the Branches Grow From Here?*

| For Future Family Members | Fill In Below |
|---|---|
| **Name Relationship to Papu My** | ________________________________ |
| **Dreams / Goals What I Am Grateful** | _________ |
| **For From Papu's Legacy** | ________________________________ |
| **Photo Box** *(Insert Photo Here)* | _________ |
| | ________________________________ |
| | _________ |
| | ________________________________ |
| | _________ |

# Epilogue – Where Love Continues

I once thought this book would end with your passing.
But now I see — there is no ending... only continuation.

Your legacy didn't end with your final breath.
It lives in every person you helped, every hand you held, every smile you gave, every prayer you whispered.

It lives...in all of us.

As long as we tell your stories — you are still here.
As long as we love the way you loved — you are still teaching.
As long as we see life through grateful eyes — you are still guiding.

Heaven gained you — but earth still carries your echo.

Every sunrise reminds me:
you are not gone.
You have simply gone ahead.

Made in the USA
Coppell, TX
18 February 2026

71898770R00075